Stephen Woodhams

stephen woodhams

portfolio of

contemporary

gardens

with special photography by

andrew wood

quadrille

*'For Mum and Dad, who have given me
constant support and encouragement
to continue with all that I believe in.'*

First published in 1999 by
Quadrille Publishing Limited
Alhambra House
27–31 Charing Cross Road
London WC2H 0LS

Editorial Director Jane O'Shea
Creative Director Mary Evans
Art Director Françoise Dietrich
Picture Researcher Nadine Bazar
Production Vincent Smith, Julie Hadingham

British Library Cataloguing-in-Publication Data
A catalogue record for this book is available
from the British Library.

ISBN 1 902757 05 X

Printed in Hong Kong

contents

foreword   6

part 1: *fusion*   22
introduction   24
defining space   26
creating mood   34
framework   40
colour & texture   48

part 2: *realization*   56
introduction   58
horizon   60
sanctuary   76
minimal   90
sensory experience   106
inside out   122
airspace   136

part 3: *directory*   150
boundaries & screens   152
surfaces   158
features   162
outside living   169
100 key plants   174

suppliers & useful addresses   185
index   188
acknowledgements   191

foreword

If you were to ask me what inspires my garden designs, I would tell you that they are fuelled by a fusion of ideas. My imagination is fired by many different aspects of the natural world, such as dramatic landscapes, the play of light, the way plants grow in their native habitat, colours and reflections in water. The historic gardens of many cultures are also a rich source of ideas and, at the other end of the timescale, I am both excited and inspired by the latest materials produced by cutting-edge technology.

For as long as I can remember I have been fascinated by modern architecture and design. I draw a great deal of inspiration from buildings such as the Getty Museum in Los Angeles, the Guggenheim in Bilbao and the renovated Reichstag building in Berlin. To my mind, these are the modern wonders of the world. It was the shape of the Grande Arche at La Défense in Paris which gave me the idea for a water feature (see page 10).

Following the example of some of the great architectural and landscape collaborations of the past, such as Capability Brown and Vanbrugh, Edwin Lutyens and Gertrude Jekyll, garden designers are once again working hand-in-hand with architects to link buildings closely with their surroundings. Sir Norman Foster, the prestigious British architect,is designing one of Europe's largest private building projects for Mclarens, owners of the Formula One racing team. The project encompasses an ecologically friendly new technology centre and an 80-hectare (200-acre) park which will feature landscaped walks, water and woodland areas to provide habitats for newly introduced wildlife. Work on this scale parallels that of the palatial country houses of the eighteenth century, such as Blenheim in Oxfordshire and Holkham in Norfolk, where Capability Brown's grassy parkland and rounded slopes swept the countryside right up to the house. It is particularly pleasing that a member of the industry blamed for some of the worst pollution in the world should be creating an ecologically friendly environment inspired by eighteenth-century garden design. Green activists and green policies have now made us so aware of our environment that our primitive desire to change our surroundings is being replaced by a wish to preserve and restore.

Although I tend to draw my inspiration from vast landscapes, grand gardens and monumental buildings, this does not mean that my own work is necessarily on such a scale. The principles work just as well when applied to more intimate spaces. Not every garden has the benefit of a fine vista, and sometimes it is necessary to draw the eye away from the boundaries and concentrate on what lies within. I consider the Japanese to be masters of this art - their minimalist Zen gardens may be composed of nothing more than a few large stones and raked gravel in an enclosed courtyard, but one cannot fail to recognize that this simple arrangement has been inspired by the island mountains which rise dramatically from the seas surrounding Japan. The minimalist garden often reinvents the bigger picture on an intimate scale without losing any of the power of the image (see page 14). Similarly, ancient Chinese gardens are whole landscapes in miniature and the Mogul gardens of India, of which the Taj Mahal is an outstanding example, sought to do nothing less than recreate Paradise on earth.

Although inspired by the past as well as the present, my gardens are very much a product of their time. I am fascinated by the juxtaposition of new industrial materials with traditional ones such as limestone and slate. I find this aspect of contemporary gardening very exciting. As well as combining the old and the new, I like to use materials which have until recently been thought of as purely utilitarian. Galvanized pots have become very much part of my trademark; I love to use them with other materials which I feel are harsh and cutting-edge, such as metal grille or non-slip metal safety flooring. I even use ordinary dustbins as giant planters, with holes drilled in the bottom for drainage.

Glass has made more impact than any other material on my own garden designs. With new technology it has become safe, durable and extremely versatile. Silicone bonding now eliminates the need for a metal framework for a conservatory or even the frameless fishtank on page 18, where the fish appear to be swimming in mid-air among grasses, irises and other spiky foliage.

In essence, my designs are a physical combination of all these different thoughts and emotions. I see them as an expression of love for what is past and of excitement about the present. While responding to the reality of contemporary life, I seek to acknowledge our intellectual debt to the garden designers of the past.

<u>above</u>
The massive structure of
La Grande Arche at La
Défense near Paris is an
example of architecture
as a potent source of
inspiration for my
own designs.

<u>above right</u>
Change of scale: the clean
lines of La Grande Arche
provided inspiration for
this water feature which
I built in a client's
garden (see page 98).

architecture

I have always drawn inspiration from the clean, untrammelled lines of contemporary buildings. When I design a garden I like to create shapes and forms that reflect this modern, architectural style. This effect can be achieved equally well through hard landscaping, planting, or a combination of both. By adopting this approach to my gardens, I add a sculptural dimension to their design. Reflecting the architectural style of the building in my design for its garden is a way of ensuring that there is a strong and coherent link between the two.

above
Nebelgarten, an exhibit
at the seventh Festival
International des Jardins
de Chaumont-sur-Loire, in
France. Using limestone
and steam, the artist has
produced something of the
effect of a geyser.

above right
Andy Goldsworthy's
*Balanced Rocks – Morecambe
Bay, May 1978.* This
landscape sculpture
highlights the beauty
of the rock forms.

nature

Nature cannot be excluded from even the most hard-line contemporary garden designs. However determined we are to dominate her, she will reassert herself. I try to work with nature in my gardens and also enjoy imitating natural effects. The natural environment often proves to be a rich source of inspiration. For example, the limestone slabs (left) are laid in a spiral, a form which frequently occurs in nature. Andy Goldsworthy's playful screen of balanced rocks evokes the fragmented stone walls left behind by earlier civilizations. It also draws our attention to the intrinsic beauty of natural, uncut rock.

scale

Garden designers love to play with scale. In the New York garden shown above right, Martha Schwartz has reinterpreted exquisite mountain-island scenery into a minimalist design. A shift in scale opens up the exciting possibility of reproducing any natural landscape within the confines of the garden. It is the islands that lend scale to the massive expanse of water, just as in Zen Buddhist gardens large stones lend scale to areas of gravel.

<u>above</u>
This rock structure, in
the gardens of the Getty
Center in Los Angeles,
has been made to look like
a naturally occurring
feature.

<u>above right</u>
Diane Edmund's *Reeds* at
the Dyson factory in
Malmesbury, Wiltshire.
Here art has been made to
imitate nature, without
the traditional pretence
of a 'natural' result
(see also page 33).

art

Ever since the Renaissance, garden designers have been playing with the relationship
between art and nature. In the past art has often been made to imitate nature so skilfully
that no one could tell the two apart. This process has been carried to a further level of
sophistication in the contemporary garden. Nobody could mistake the fibre optic lights in
the photograph above for real plants, but by placing them in water, the artist has created
a witty, synthetic imitation of a real, rush-filled pool.

A silicone-bonded glass
aquarium, exhibited at
the Chaumont garden
festival, creates an
ethereal impression.

above right
This glass gazebo,
designed by architects
Brookes Stacey Randall,
exploits the natural
advantages of its site.

materials

Designers have access to an enormous range of highly sophisticated materials, many of them used in industry and architecture. Glass is particularly versatile and allows a spontaneous blurring of the boundary between interior and exterior spaces. In a magical fusion of elements, these glazed structures appear to be suspended between sky and earth, scarcely interrupting the view: the aquarium on the left is almost invisible and the fish appear to be suspended in mid-air. By using glass as their main material they have detracted nothing from the beautiful view of the river.

landscape

When I design a garden I want it to be a part of the landscape that surrounds it. At the same time, I want to make a mark upon that landscape. Designers have always used the vista as a means of imposing their will upon the landscape. Although they do not touch the natural scenery, they frame it in such a way that it becomes a part of their own design. This technique is used in grand gardens such as Versailles, and in the Picturesque landscapes invented by eighteenth-century painters. The photographs shown here are examples of the way in which the same technique is still used today.

<u>defining space</u> 26

<u>creating mood</u> 34

<u>framework</u> 40

<u>colour & texture</u> 48

part 1:
fusion

previous pages
Apartment and roof terrace
by Stanton Williams; end-
on view of the pavilion
shown on page 19.

right
Carex elata in a galvan-
ized container on the
author's terrace.

24 I have always felt that there is a link between the ancient stone circles of

Stonehenge and Avebury in Wiltshire, England, and our modern gardens. The standing

stones were a way of claiming the land, establishing possession in order to use it

as a place for celebration and ritual. Today we use our gardens for less formal

purposes, yet we still collect stones and arrange them in our gardens.

In my garden designs I seek to acknowledge the ancient use of landscape while

reinterpreting it in modern form. This fusion between old and new has become one of

my trademarks.

In this part of the book I examine four aspects that I consider fundamental to

the creation of a contemporary garden. The first is space which has been deliberately

defined. Then I explain how physical elements such as plants, water and light can be

combined to create a mood or atmosphere within that space. This is followed by a

discussion of the framework and the use of colour and texture.

It is the fusion of the past and the present, the abstract and the concrete that

is at the heart of the successful design for a contemporary garden.

Making a garden is all about dividing up space. This process may create many different views, only some of which will be visible at any one time. In the great formal gardens of the past, the division was achieved with complex geometric designs set along vistas defined by topiary, fountains and parterres. Designs on this vast scale are rarely possible in contemporary gardens, but even the smallest space should have room for a single vista and, most enticing of all, a surprise view into another area.

defining space

All the traditional devices for defining space are still valid today, even though the average contemporary garden is on a much smaller scale than the grand gardens of the past. It is often made up of a mixture of formal and informal elements, for few people want the perfect symmetry that was traditionally used to define space. By including some order, however, even if it is just through repetition in the planting scheme, a sense of balance may be achieved. Space may also be defined through the placement of focal points, created perhaps by the strategic positioning of a showy plant, a piece of sculpture or a water feature. Or the eye may be channelled through an arch or an opening in a fence or trellis, and drawn to a planting or vista beyond.

rooms & views

Although open to the elements, the garden should feel like a controlled space. This space can be further defined through division into distinct areas or 'rooms'. These need not necessarily be closed off from one another, although there should be enough distinction to create the sense that you are experiencing different views. Both gardens here, one private, the other public, manage to create long vistas in relatively small spaces (see next page and pages 68–76).

<u>above</u>
The slatted table lies parallel to the sea. Led by the brick pathway and symmetrical planting, the eye is launched past the stone ball sculpture, out to the horizon.

<u>right</u>
The lines of the walls, rill and paving in Parc André Citroen, Paris, demonstrate a powerful use of perspective. This is accentuated by the dynamism of the water as it flows down the horizontal ridges in a show of air, bubbles and shadowy light.

■ A view through a wall to steps leading up to French windows is emphasized by the reflections in the water and an immensely long horizontal branch above the pool.
■ A smaller rill in the same park in Paris creates an imposing vertical as well as horizontal space as the water falls down between massive granite panels.
■ A reveal or window can be used to frame a view. Circles and oval shapes are useful for creating a soft effect; here, in a garden designed by Bob Clark, an ivy-clad oval 'window' is emphasized by the rounded glass bottle shapes, *objets trouvés* which add to the sense of mystery suggested by the strange topiary shapes in the garden beyond.

29

above
A water vista in Parc André Citroen, Paris, shown as a detail on the previous page, is seen to be a slope leading the eye firmly to a vertical tower within a transparent pavilion.

Creating views or vistas is also a means of leading the eye. When Capability Brown planted his avenues, he used only one variety of tree, a practice that reflected his understanding of perspective: he knew that repeat images irresistibly draw the eye and give the strongest sense of perspective. The same device is used in the contemporary Parc André Citroen in Paris, where the perspective is extended by the use of progressively shorter specimens of hornbeam (*Carpinus betulus*) arranged in two huge parallel plantings (see left). This has the effect of making the avenue look longer than it actually is. A glass structure forms the focal point at the far end.

By opening a view through to another, more attractive area of the garden, you can 'lose' a less appealing foreground. An effect I particularly like to use is created by constructing a square arch through which a series of repeating arches may be seen, rather like a roofless pergola. The spaces between the uprights can be planted if you wish to create a greater depth of perspective. Such an arch, carefully positioned, can be used to draw the eye

<u>above</u>
A simple planting of bright
yellow rudbeckia gains
an extra dimension when
viewed through a frame
of woven willow.

<u>left</u>
The strong shadows cast
by the slatted roof of a
Modernist-inspired gazebo
emphasize the drama of
this severe structure and
the encroaching foliage.

<u>below</u>
The alignment of the
exterior planting of olive
trees underplanted with
boxwood, the boxwood ball
in a terracotta pot, and
the jar within the room
provide an interesting
interplay between garden
and interior.

right
These angular slabs both divide and measure the length of the flat lawn, making an abstract link between the house and the wood beyond the garden. The stones have a power-ful, almost inevitable presence in their own right.

through to a particular area of the garden, framing it like a picture.

Sometimes a naturally occurring view may need to be screened. If there is an eyesore such as an ugly structure or a boundary in sight, the eye may simply be diverted by some strategic planting, like a large shrub or tree. Alternatively, screening may be used to create a sense of separation or enclosure. The screen could be a trellis clad with climbers or even a semi-transparent material such as glass or even muslin (see page 35). Garden structures made of modern materials are often easier, cheaper and quicker to construct than the traditional kind, and the fact

that they may be less solid and more temporary can be a positive advantage. It allows the division of space in the garden to be more flexible. Just as space within the rooms of a house can be changed by the furnishings, so in the garden there can be greater scope for making changes.

perspective

Tricks of perspective can be particularly useful in small gardens to give the illusion that the space is greater than it actually is. Devices such as physically narrowing a path as it recedes, or keeping background planting to misty greys and blues, will make a garden appear longer. Mirrors can

above
A daring fusion of ideas
uses rusty steel uprights
as the trunks and main
branches of man-made
trees, with suspended
plastic pipes sprouting
willow cuttings and trails
of ground ivy (*Glechoma
hederacea variegata*)
forming a foliage canopy.

right
A glass wall at the Dyson
factory, Malmesbury, makes
a mirror effect, reflecting
the sky and landscape
surroundings. The
lighting, reed sculpture,
metal bridge and railings
over the 'moated' entrance
combine to give a great
feeling of atmosphere and
depth.

be used to create a false perspective and are especially good at opening out a small space; the mirrored end to the terrace below effectively doubles its length. I placed a mirror on either side of a conservatory (see page 130), and planted the foreground with white hydrangeas; the mirrors multiplied the plants many times, giving the effect of a large, heavily planted area and making the room feel larger and less enclosed than before.

Paths are an important device in the use of perspective, as they help define space and act as an invitation to walk through the garden. The width of a path can even dictate the pace of progress. A rill of water, on the other hand, encourages a pause for thought and can play an equally strong role in creating perspective. This device dates back to early Islamic gardens, where low rectangular pools of water and fountains were linked by narrow canals.

I like to use arches or timber frames over pathways or canals. They frame the view, creating an effect similar to that of a traditional pergola. It is not always realized that a pergola has a dual effect upon perspective: it works both vertically and horizontally, creating two separate areas and the potential for two very different moods.

As you walk through a pergola each of the spaces to either side frames a different view, forming a series of changing pictures along the pathway. I have found that the apparent space may be extended by placing repeat features along the sides of the pergola. This effect is further enhanced by placing something, such as an urn or a specimen plant, at the far end of the main axis, to create a focal point.

A pergola does not have to consist of a double row of straight lines: it can be square or rectangular, giving a canopy over a wide area, or may be curved to follow a pathway. The traditional tunnel effect conjures up mystery and an interesting alteration in perspective. Planted with climbers growing up wires or trellis, the pergola can become an enclosed room. From within it feels intimate and warm, but from outside it intrigues and draws you in.

33

left
Here broad bands of sloping grass and narrow paved pathways create a bold perspective in a corner of Parc André Citroen in Paris.

Your garden design will work better if you are aware from the outset of the mood you hope to create. If you fail to define the mood of the garden, you may find yourself tempted to include elements which will work against the main theme. In reaching your decision, remember that the contemporary garden should pander to all the senses — sight, sound, touch, smell and even taste.

creating mood

A successful garden always has a distinctive atmosphere. The creation of this atmosphere should be a key consideration for anyone designing a new garden. To some extent, the mood of the garden may dictate the way in which it is used. For example, you may want to create a garden which will encourage contemplation and you should ensure that each element of the design is sympathetic to this aim. You might plant aromatic species along the paths so that they release their fragrance when brushed against. Their scent and the rich texture of their leaves will tempt the passer-by to linger. Grasses and bamboos will rustle gently in the breeze, creating a sense of place that you can appreciate even with your eyes closed.

By including water in the garden you will immediately define its mood and create an atmosphere. The sight and

left
Water glides down granite pavers in an enclosure at Parc André Citroen to collect in a V-shaped trough. The sound evokes a natural cascade, and, in masking the city noise, creates a perfect place for contemplation.

<u>above</u>

An installation from the Chaumont garden festival: a framework covered in white gauze with twining plants such as morning glory clambering over it takes on the appearance of a lush tropical environment as the mist system fills the early-morning air with fine water droplets.

left
Surprise is an important element in a garden. Here a gatepost is topped with pieces of crystal from an old chandelier. They are illuminated from above by a simple outdoor light bulb hung in the tree.

below
Drilled pebbles mounted on metal rods are planted in a sinuous ribbon among drifts of statice and grasses. They make a tapping sound and create a wonderful feeling of movement, with grasses blowing in the breeze.

right
A collection of sea-washed pebbles and shells with natural holes in them have been threaded onto a string. A memento of a seaside visit, they capture the magic of the day they were collected.

sound of water comfort the spirit. Looking down into still water is cool and relaxing, and the play of light and the reflections are somehow satisfying and reassuring. The sound of gently moving water can be especially soothing – particularly if it blocks out other, less welcome background noises. On the other hand, a large, gushing water feature can have the opposite effect on the atmosphere of the garden, generating a sense of drama, excitement or even alarm.

lighting the set

Lighting will enable you to conjure up a mood that is almost theatrical. I have seen chandelier crystals hung high in the trees and lit at night, the sparkling crystals reflected in mirrors hung from the branches. Although I found the effect rather threatening, it was strangely charming, like an outdoor set for *A Midsummer Night's Dream*.

How you light – or don't light – your garden plays a vital part in evoking its atmosphere at night. I never use flood-lights as they make the garden feel very flat and uninviting. Lighting should be all about creating mystery and surprise, as well as defining what I call 'hot' and 'cold' areas. By this I mean having focused light, such as a spotlight, on a specific feature like a shrub, a tree or a statue, and then having softer, diffused light, such as candlelight, placed around a table used for entertaining. Where possible I also like to use back-lighting behind a table – perhaps along a screen or a wall of ivy – to create a greater sense of depth.

This garden sets out to summon up a sleepy South-ern or sunny Mediterranean atmosphere. White awnings, light paving, warm terra-cotta pots, reclining chairs and plants such as olive trees achieve the effect.

left
A black net pergola, like an octagonal outdoor room, has an exotic appeal.

the exotic

39

What you find exotic depends on where you live and who you are. Materials of all kinds can play a strong part in helping to create an exotic mood, and plants are particu-larly important here.

You might, for example, want to create a Mediterranean feeling in your cool-climate garden, which could be achieved by planting a pencil-thin line of Italian cypresses. In one garden, I used planters of standard olive trees and rendered the walls in a light honey-grey colour. Because the tones of the render and the foliage were so similar, they gave a real sense of a garden in the hot, dry South of France, an association amplified by the use of pleached limes to mark two perimeter boundaries (see page 85).

For centuries gardens have been a meeting point for different cultures. This cultural fusion can be reflected in exotic planting or in forms and ideas borrowed from the architectural vocabulary of other cultures. We are now so used to seeing bamboos in our gardens that we are apt to forget that they are sub-tropical plants from East and Southeast Asia. Nevertheless, they still conjure up an East-meets-West feel when incorporated into planting or hard landscaping.

above
A feeling of calm is engendered by the welcome shade of a lovely old olive tree at this house designed by Claudio Silvestrin. There is a repeated use of strong horizontals and verticals in the steps, the stone benches and slabs as well as in the dining recess.

The contemporary fashion for minimalist gardens has made the creation of a proper framework more important than ever. Bold architecture is the keynote of contemporary garden design and both plants and man-made structures may be used to create curves or straight lines. Like a modern building, the garden's architecture encompasses 'voids', such as lawns or gravel areas, as well as the more obvious vertical features.

framework

The topiary shapes used to create a screen on this roof terrace have a reassuring and protective presence.

This garden at Erigny, Périgord (recreated recently from an eighteenth-century design) could have inspired the roof garden above.

top
An aerial photograph of a parterre reveals the dramatic effect which can be achieved by restricting planting to one type of shrub.

above
An interesting use of shapes and textures: standard topiary balls of privet (*Ligustrum*) are mirrored at ground level by hummocks of *Berberis thunbergii* f. *atropurpurea* with contrasting purple foliage, echoed in the sage underplanting.

In the contemporary garden, planting is used in conjunction with hard landscaping to give the garden its framework or architectural quality. This approach to garden design has a history stretching back over thousands of years. In the magnificent gardens of the Roman emperors, the strong shapes of topiary, pergolas, arcades and ornate and patterned planting made a framework for the entire garden site.

Powerful, geometric plant forms are still popular in gardens today, where they are used to create and underpin a bold, structural framework. Ground surface shapes made from paving and grass are also deployed to make strong structural statements from which the style of the rest of the site will follow. Once this framework is established, form and pattern offer scope for sheer theatre.

The planting plan of a contemporary garden can be designed either to echo or to contrast with the architecture that it surrounds. A modern house consisting of straight-edged uprights and horizontals without curves can have its severity emphasized by planting designed around straight lines and square blocks of well-clipped plants. Alternatively the garden could be planted in a more fluid fashion, using the flowing forms of artemisia and lavender to soften the

left
Verticals can be used to
make a pleasing pattern
as well as to define space.
In this garden designed
by Arabella Lennox-Boyd,
the upright trunks of the
pleached limes contrast
pleasingly with the rect-
angular water feature.

left
The upright columns of
a pavilion in this garden
designed by Jeff Mendoza
work well with plant
textures and shapes and
frame the 'soft' sculpture
of a large green bird.

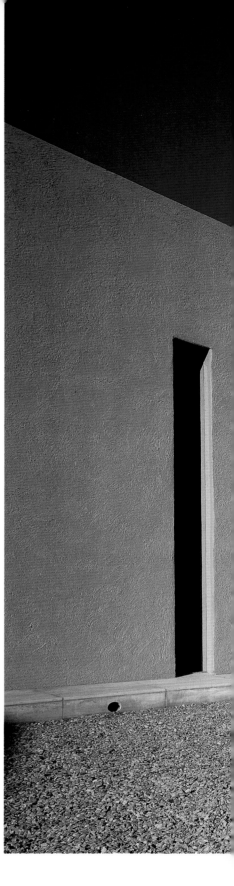

42 edges of the architectural blocks. Low swathes of planting
look good when punctuated by tall, columnar, structural
plants such as *Juniperus scopulorum* 'Skyrocket', a
blue-green conifer than never gets wider than 40–50cm
(18–20in) and grows to about 5m (16ft) tall. Three of them
together look very impressive.

planting patterns

By limiting plant varieties to five or less, the form and
pattern of a planting plan are strengthened. I like the sense
of geometry and containment that such an arrangement
gives. I will choose plants that can be close-clipped, such
as yew or rosemary, as they are in keeping with the
severity of such a layout. For a touch of informality, I would
also include plant groupings that lend a softer, looser
appearance: lavender, purple sage (*Salvia officinalis*
'Purpurascens') or cotton lavender (*Santolina chamaecyparissus*) for instance. Hedging plants can be used to form
strong, graphic patterns in the garden, especially when
they are clipped into topiary shapes. The most effective
hedges consist of a single evergreen variety such as yew,
box or privet, although deciduous plants such as beech,
and hornbeam also shape easily.

<u>above</u>

A fine example of just how simple a house and garden can be. The house has minimal square windows and a long, narrow entrance to let in light. The oversized palms look impressively structural in this setting and the honey-coloured gravel and limestone walkway tone harmoniously with the painted exterior. At night the trunks of the palms are strikingly illuminated by uplighters.

When I choose plants it is not exclusively for their beautiful form, colour or scent. I try to visualize their very essence so that I can picture exactly what each one might contribute to the overall character and structure of the garden. In other words, I don't think of the plant in isolation but I see it as one of the many elements that make up an artistic installation.

fluid forms

It is possible to create the effect of flowing water by planting a single variety of a silver-leaved plant in batches, and slightly altering the level between one batch and another. This is a useful visual trick on a sloping site. When choosing your plants, it is important to remember the way they alter from season to season. This will enable you to plan a design which changes gradually throughout the course of the year.

Monochrome plantings can be used to strengthen the framework of the garden. By using very large drifts of one

44

left

A curved wall in a London park encloses a play area. The semi-circular planting of *Brachyglottis greyi* at its base matches the pattern and tone of the sloping bank of cobbles beautifully. The path is set in concrete blocks, edged with bricks and granite pavers.

left

Broad avenues and narrower pathways edged in plaited willow screens create unusual ground patterns. The place and the experience are transformed by the sense of mystery and revelation that the screens impart.

<u>above</u>

Pathways of grey pebbles in a maze-like pattern lead the traveller to an oasis consisting of a pool of clear water encircled by a woven willow screen. Surrounding beds of richly coloured dahlias thrive, as if taking their nourishment from the hidden oasis.

type of plant, with only slight variations in colour, I can also create an impression of overwhelming abundance. This is especially pronounced when using highly scented flowers, such as intoxicating lilies or musky roses.

Sometimes you may need only one or two plant varieties to create a garden that will make an immediate and striking impression on first-time visitors. I call this giving a garden the 'Wow' factor. Restricting your approach to planting in this way can also help to create an exciting feeling of space.

solid forms

Not for me the unfettered patchwork of a traditional country garden – I would rather have a garden clad with limestone paving, a bench and two plain stone pots, one planted with a *Cedrus atlantica* f. *glauca*, topped with pebbles and the other with a mound of *Festuca glauca*.

I love curved walls and I especially appreciate the one at the recently restored London park, in Kensal Road, W10, designed by Charles Voysey in the early 1900s, in which a play park featuring a curved yellow wall has been added to

right
Boundaries can set the tone of a garden. Here a curving metal fence in the Voysey park accent‑uates the wavy bed and its border of cobbles.

below right
In this natural woodland‑edge setting, an unusual boundary looks completely in keeping. Here Andy Goldsworthy's *The Wall went for a Walk* at Grizedale in Cumbria snakes sensuously around the trees.

left
A long, curving wall, designed by Martha Schwarz, studded with coloured glass portholes follows the contours of this lush, grassy site. Wall and ground provide the perfect flowing organic backdrop for the specimen tree in the foreground, a simple but exciting juxtaposition that could be used on a smaller scale in a garden.

the original layout (see page 44). The Voysey park is also an example of the way in which old-fashioned paving methods can be given a contemporary interpretation. For example, there are areas where pebbles have been set on edge in flowing, curved mortar shapes. I recently used pebbles on edge to surface an area between some highly polished glass-fibre planters and the lovely, square lime-stone paving on a roof garden. The effect was further enhanced by a planting of informal, silver-toned plants, echoing the colour of the pebbles and making a pleasing

contrast with the crisp lines of the planters (see page 110).

Traditional fencing materials may be abandoned in favour of stainless steel, another feature of the carefully designed framework at the Voysey park. Here, the effect is softened by the use of patterned panels in wonderfully 'organic' forms and powder-coated, coloured sections.

By limiting the range of plants and the variety of hard surfaces used, you restrict the palette – or shades of colour – to quite a narrow range. This is where texture becomes important, particularly in small garden areas where you tend to see plants and surfaces close up. It does not, however, mean that you are denied the impact of strong colour contrasts and explosive effects.

colour & texture

My sense of colour works at two different levels. On the one hand I use a near-monochromatic range so that there is scope for appreciating every subtle change of hue, while on the other I sometimes create a riot of colour, indulging the visual sense to the full.

I tend to choose hard surfaces and planting from within the same tonal range; this has the effect of making each colour work harder, whether it is a muted green or cream, or the brightest pink or orange. In a subtle design, the colour scheme may start with raised beds rendered in a creamy grey finish to harmonize with York stone paving. This will then be teamed with highly textured plants with greenish-grey, silver and dark green foliage, such as olive trees, box, *Euphorbia characias* subsp. *wulfenii*, *Artemisia*

'Powis Castle' and *Santolina incana*, all of which have wonderful silver-grey tones. For me these plants conjure up images of shimmering heat, perhaps arid desert palms or scrub, or even the South of France with its hazy, Mediterranean warmth. In cooler climates all these muted colours need is a little sunshine to bring them alive.

I invariably plant shaded areas of a garden with a range of green foliage plants. These are generally the easiest plants to grow in dry or moist shade and often, like the ivies and some ferns, have shiny surfaces that reflect light. I love to add some white-flowered plants such as white foxgloves (*Digitalis purpurea* f. *alba*), *Trillium grandiflorum* or white hellebores (*Helleborus orientalis*) as they add luminosity to the planting by reflecting what little light there is.

far left
A weathered bamboo fence in tones of honey and grey provides a dappled backdrop for a shocking-pink azalea. Unexpected use of colour and texture are defining aspects of good garden design.

left
This chequered planting scheme is interesting not only because of its textures, but also because the colour combinations work so well — especially the silver-grey echeveria which brings out the pink tones of the gravel.

right
In this courtyard of a house by Luis Barragan the colour has been intensified by the textured finish of the wall and by its conjunction with the black inner courtyard floor, which is a water feature. A collection of terracotta pots relieves the intensity of the 'hot' colour and tones well with the terracotta shard floor.

<u>left</u>
The rough texture of the wall, the spiky foliage and the desiccated trunk of the yucca conjure up images of hot, sunny climates and open spaces, without losing the intimate association of texture and colour.

<u>right</u>
Here the impression is of muted sandy colours and textures: the simple modern lines of buildings combine with organic curves in a design by Bonita Bulaitis that is softened by informal grasses and purple-flowered *Verbena bonariensis*.

<u>above</u>
This garden, of a building by Valode and Pistre, has a more polished and precise feel with assorted, yet controlled, textures in green and white.

I consider texture to be almost as important as colour, especially when working within a limited palette. Take silver and grey tones: the colour variation may be slight, but when texture is taken into account there is an exciting diversity. There are, for example, the dramatic webbed leaves of *Cynara cardunculus*, the furry leaves of verbascum, the finely dissected foliage of *Santolina chamaecyparissus* and the sparkle of water on the blue-tinged leaves of the coral plume (*Macleaya cordata*). Lamb's ears (*Stachys byzantina*) has silky hairs covering its felty leaves, making it irresistible.

Wherever possible, introduce plants with tactile qualities into the garden. Trees with interesting bark, such as the paper-bark maple (*Acer griseum*), *Prunus serrula* and *Betula utilis* or even the magnificent *Magnolia grandiflora*, whose leaves are glossy on top with suede undersides, should be sought out and included in your planting plan. Then there are the grasses, which look good all year round. Both the leaves and the seedheads invite touch and the previous year's growth looks wonderful in mid-winter.

hot colour

I think strong colours are here to stay. I admire designers like Topher Delaney and Luis Barragan (see page 49) who

■ Suspended stained-glass panels bring another element of colour into this garden by Jonathan Baillie. The golden hop contrasts well with the glass.

■ The use of an accent colour can make a very effective statement within a plain garden.

■ The singular beauty of a solitary red bloom among a sea of green lily pads demands attention.

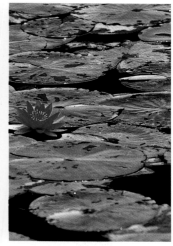

<u>right</u>
The silver and grey hard landscaping in this garden offsets the orange and red planting so that everything, including the parasol, contributes to the overall effect.

52

make use of painted walls and screens; we haven't seen such a wave of colour on either side of the Atlantic since the designs of Gertrude Jekyll with her orange, red and yellow borders. Until now, gardeners in northerly latitudes tended to play safe and keep to a country-garden palette of pink, blue and white, although Christopher Lloyd, in his garden at Great Dixter in Sussex, England, has always been an advocate of the daring use of colour.

It is to the Mediterranean and the southern climes of America that one usually looks for vibrant colour and lush, tropical plants. Strong colours work best in bright sunlight, or in the dramatic and colourful cactus gardens found in California and New Mexico.

The whole subject of colour theory is fascinating. I find that I am being drawn increasingly towards hot colours, which may be the result of growing confidence, allowing me to be bolder in my use of colour. It is interesting to observe that many gardeners believe red to be a difficult colour to use, despite the fact that it is directly opposite green in the colour wheel and therefore 'complementary' to it. Personally I think that red should be used more. There is a lot of red in some of my favourite foliage plants: *Berberis thunbergii* f. *atropurpurea*, *Salvia officinalis* 'Purpurascens'

and bronze fennel. I love placing red among other strong colours like orange, purple and yellow, or even brown. The combination can be very exciting, but be warned: it is not a colour scheme for the faint-hearted.

Sometimes colour schemes can be created inadvertently: a chosen variety of plant may not be available and so a substitute is found. If you are lucky, the result may even be an improvement on the original scheme. Accidental associations may also occur. I recall admiring the red timbers in the entrance of a house, next to a lovely red-leafed maple in a terracotta pot. However, it was the chance placing of a large golden-leafed maple that completed the picture by bringing the reds to life and picking up on the yellow tones.

At the moment I am experimenting with copper as the basis for a palette – I mean both the metal and the foliage and flowers in lovely, earthy browns and oranges – with a touch of feathery silver and grey. I find yellow, on the other hand, a tricky colour to use. I think that it really only looks good in a mass planting of one variety, such as narcissi or daffodils in the spring. That said, I love to see the crinkly ribbon-like strands of *Hamamelis mollis* on a winter's day – its colour is so crisp and the flowers amazingly fragrant.

fusion

above
In this courtyard garden
by Tom Hobbs, there is
a perfect interplay of
colour and texture. The
orange-pink walls are
a warm backdrop to the
grey paving and the
silver-grey planting
scheme, with its orange
and purple accents.

right
An accidental but
perfect fusion of colour
and texture – the strap-
like leaves of the red
phormium are intersected
by a bare branch which
emphasizes the rigidity
of form and the colour of
the background plant.

below
The hot pink geraniums
in the foreground link
nicely with the willow-
weave fence panels and
the feathery foliage of
the *Acer palmatum* beyond.

The use of strong colours is not restricted to the plants in a garden. At the Chaumont garden festival in France I was inspired by a garden designed to resemble a dried-up river bed (see page 64). Organic swathes of planting were interspersed with various pieces of debris, all of it painted red, apparently deposited after a flood. The colour and positioning of the objects eloquently symbolized the unpredictable nature of a river and its hidden dangers.

On a smaller scale, an interesting effect can be achieved by painting just one wall of a terrace area with a bright colour. I have seen a rendered wall painted hot pink, providing a perfect backdrop for architectural plants. When planning to use strong colour on the hard surfaces in your garden it is wise to do a bit of experimenting first. Colours can be altered at different times of day and in changing lights. Paint some test boards and position them against the surface you are planning to paint, to get an idea of the effect and to see exactly how the colour changes throughout the day.

Choosing a colour theme for a garden is ultimately about personal taste. What you may consider to be a wonderful colour combination may be perceived as a totally confused picture by someone else, but since it is your garden, it should be planned first and foremost for your own pleasure.

<u>horizon</u>   60

<u>sanctuary</u>   76

<u>minimal</u>   90

<u>sensory experience</u>   106

<u>inside out</u>   122

<u>airspace</u>   136

part 2:
realization

realization

right
A carpet of box (*Buxus
sempervirens*) in giant
cast-aluminium pots at
London's elegant One
Aldwych hotel; the pots
are uplit at night. I love
to 'reverse' scale like
this when I can.

58 Having defined the contemporary garden as a fusion of different intellectual ideas
and physical forms, we progress in this part of the book to an examination of the
way in which these elements can be realized in a specific site.

This part of the book falls into six sections. In each one I look at a different
aspect of design. The topics that I cover have been triggered by gardens of my own
design and each section includes a project garden of particular relevance to that
topic. My own intimate knowledge of these gardens has made it possible for me to
describe the whole design process, from the initial site visit and client 'wish
list' to the final realization of the design. An annotated site plan adds further
detail to the information about each site.

previous pages
Seascape from the beach
garden featured on pages
68-75; minimalist plant-
ing of a traditional
parterre harmonizes with
the open country-house
setting.

horizon

In a confined urban context the garden's horizon may stretch only as far as the rear wall of a neighbouring house, whereas in a more open setting it may share the horizon with the surrounding landscape. In some cases the horizon is limited by a beautiful feature such as a large tree, while in others it may encompass a fine view of a city park, distant fields and hills or the sea beyond the garden boundary. To shut out these natural assets would be to waste a glorious opportunity.

above
Architect Richard Meier's incredible ridge-top ramparts at the Getty Center stretch vistas over Los Angeles and to the distant horizon. The gardens are filled with cacti and succulents.

left
Minimalist furnishings and strongly horizontal garden structures are in keeping with the setting's undulating landscape. The lines of the wide, low table top take the eye over the loggia and into the hills; I especially like the pots of phormiums and the chairs arranged in series of three.

When we acquire a garden or piece of land, most of us think first of enclosing it. This achieves a measure of privacy and establishes it as our property. But before creating a boundary, it is vital to consider the natural horizon of the site, and to decide whether you want to screen it out or to incorporate it into your garden design.

If you decide to draw the horizon into your garden, colour or form may be used to create a visual link between the area of enclosure and the landscape beyond. I once designed a garden in which I used the theme of yellow gorse on a nearby hillside to marry with bright yellow-glazed pots which were planted with *Hosta sieboldiana* and placed on the terrace. I also remember a garden in the Napa Valley in California where lines of lavender bushes planted around the swimming pool area reflected the rows of grape vines on the surrounding hills. This device emphasized the beauty of the vines while making a satisfying link between hillside and garden, not as easy as it seems.

A mirror-effect similar to that described above can also be created on a vertical axis. In this case, a single arch or tree can be used to reflect the uprights, such as tree trunks, in the wider landscape. Naturally, it is easier to make visual links of this kind when the garden is sited in

These screens, by architect Claudio Silvestrin, draw your eye along the path towards the distant horizon, through a secondary wall. A centrally positioned uplighter emphasizes the narrow gap in the screens when they are seen at night from the other side.

above
Olive trees disguise the existing boundaries in this garden, leading the eye to a neighbouring building. This use of 'borrowed landscape' creates a sense of space.

above
Californian landscape architect Ron Lutsko has used a narrow canal to lead the eye to the horizon. The effect is strengthened by interesting planting.

undulating, open country, but it can be done on a balcony or roof garden, too. This idea of creating an 'open' horizon works well with the contemporary preference for a minimal style. With planting and structures simplified to a few graphic strokes, there is little to interrupt a framed view along a vista, or the upward pull of a strong vertical.

I particularly admire designers who are able to create a seamless link with the surrounding countryside. One such design appears on page 64, where Ron Lutsko has made use of a screen of tall grasses. By incorporating features from the garden's surroundings into your design you are using what is known as 'borrowed landscape'. If you plan to do this, a traditional wall, hedge or fence may not be the most appropriate boundary and a less intrusive, transparent screen might well be the answer.

In gardens such as the one shown on page 120, neighbours may come to a mutual agreement to take down a shared wall in order to keep the boundary as fluid as possible. In this case, the trees in a neighbouring garden could become an important part of your own horizon.

Even if you have a boundary around your garden, you can build up layers of planting to soften it, reducing the sense of enclosure and making it possible to 'borrow' surrounding scenery. The secret is to build up gradually from small ground-cover plants to semi-mature herbaceous plants, and then to use shrubs and larger trees to direct the eye towards the skyline.

Some time ago, I was asked to create a strong link between a client's garden and the communal woodland beyond. We also had to provide privacy and a sufficient variety of plants to convey a sense of the changing seasons. The boundary was marked by a wrought iron balustrade overhung by mature trees. We soon covered this over with a large-leaved ivy which thrived in the deep

far left
In a garden designed to resemble a dried-up river bed, you can view a man-made horizon of layered plants which grow taller towards the back; with the arch, they give a sense of perspective.

left
Designer Ron Lutsko used swathes of grasses and mounds of santolina and lavender to echo the blue hills of the Napa Valley.

64

shade cast by the trees. We introduced some reasonably mature evergreens in the form of 5m- (16ft-) high bay trees (*Laurus nobilis*) and a pyramid *Magnolia grandiflora* and a long-needled pine, both of similar heights. These provided the crucial screening and a strong, year-round effect to stand against the backdrop of mature trees in the woodland (see page 93). The layered planting device described above could also be used to divert the eye from an ugly building on the garden's horizon.

Creating vistas that direct the eye beyond the confines of the garden is another way of extending the perceived space of the site. The view may be framed by screens or wall panels positioned in such a way that they direct the eye towards the horizon. This is the device used in the court-yard of a house in Mallorca, shown on page 62. Screens are equally useful for partially blocking the line of sight, which has the effect of diverting the eye up to the sky.

By turning the view skywards you can also compensate for the lack of a distant horizon. The eye may also be drawn away from a dead end and towards the sky by clever planting or the strategic placing of garden struc-tures. This same effect is obtained by the row of mophead palms striding across the horizon in the garden shown on page 66.

A strong visual lead may be created with water or with a path, whether it is straight or gently meandering. A path may be sited to take in secondary views of neighbouring gardens to either side of the site. Even in a very small garden, it is nearly always possible to create a short vista. If you are completely hemmed in by high buildings, however, you could try using mirrors to lgive the illusion of space, as in the garden on pages 130-5.

A stretch of still water creates the same sense of space as a mirror, as it reflects the surroundings and the sky. It doesn't need to be large – the small rill seen on the previous page is ideal. Its strong perspective leads the eye away into the distance. The best reflections are obtained using black or grey pool liner, rather than blue.

<u>above</u>
Water helps to bring a sense
of space into the garden
as it reflects the sky.
'Tame' garden palms are
included in a design by
Steve Chase to echo the
wild palms in the landscape.

realization

<u>below left</u>
Defining boundaries can
create interesting hori-
zons. Here mophead palms
dance along the ridge,
echoing both the roofline
of a building designed by
Richard Neutra and the
grass steps leading up to
the swimming pool.

<u>below right</u>
On to eternity: here is a
good example of planting
which takes the eye to
the horizon. The plants
build up a flow of
texture, colour and shape
for the eye to follow.

When I was thinking about the design for the perimeter
edge for the seaside garden shown below right and
featured on the following pages, I knew that I wanted to
retain its openness. I loved the feeling of 'garden into landscape' and wanted to create the sense that the view went
on for ever, peaceful and uninterrupted. At the same time
I wanted boundaries that would give structure and protection for the exposed seaside site, as well as a feeling of
strength and continuity.

Stretched along the beach were timber groynes, put
there to contain the rolling mass of pebbles. It was these
groynes that inspired me to use hurdles made of woven
willow to protect the planting. Low hurdles gave shelter to
the borders and higher ones acted as screens for the new
plantings of pine trees. The result is a garden that takes its
lead from the natural landscape – the expanse of sea and
sky that gives way to the most amazing horizon with its
ever-changing light.

<u>right</u>
The swimming pool of the
Neutra house (seen far
left). When you are dealing
with such a vast horizon
as the sea, screens
narrow the view without
spoiling it. Here the harsh-
ness of the walls is a
good foil for the natural
softness of the sand dunes.
The walls also give
protection, so that
bougainvillea grows
freely here.

beach vista

<u>from left</u>
- Slatted teak furniture, in groups of three, keeps the garden's look cool and simple.
- Temporary high wicker screens protect newly planted young pine trees.
- A low recliner ensures that the view across the garden is uninterrupted.

Here a flat, almost square garden fully exploits its wonderful position overlooking the sea. Raised a mere 2m (6ft) above the beach, it is exposed to the sea to the south, while fenced boundaries to either side adjoin neighbours' gardens. From the house, a pair of doors opens onto a brick terrace facing the sea.

left
The view along the garden's main vista is stopped midway by a shallow stone urn containing spheres of pumice stone. Beyond it the eye is allowed to wander out to sea.

below, from left
■ The old wall has been given new life with alternating plantings of santolina and blocks of white pebbles.
■ Low willow hurdles protect the beds and echo the lines of the groynes.
■ A view from the house to the Lutyens-style seat, forming a focal point along a side vista.
■ Looking the other way, from the recliner to the line of sheltering pine trees.

Leading from the terrace is a central pathway in matching brick, which divides the garden into two roughly equal parts. I fell for its nicely weathered rows of old bricks pointing out to the far horizon beyond the sea, which led me to make this thoroughly traditional feature into the starting point for a complete overhaul of the design.

From the main path a flight of steps leads directly down to the beach; to either side is the sloping sea defence wall. When you stand on the terrace, the sea reflects the colour of the sky and the view along the path looks as though it continues for ever. Halfway along, the path widens to form a crossing point, where secondary vistas lead to the side boundaries. One of these views is stopped by an elegant garden seat. The midpoint is marked by a shallow stone urn set on a plinth; it had been planted earlier in the year. Along

left

I had to create a means of protecting the planting from sea winds. My inspiration came from the wooden groynes that run down into the water at regular intervals. I placed woven willow panels along the sea wall and around the square sections of planting to mirror the groynes and emphasize the garden's symmetry.

either side of the path were two thin, rectangular borders edged with stone.

Our brief was to extend the flower beds along the path and in front of the house, and to incorporate a more varied selection of plants to give effect for most of the year. We needed to provide windbreaks for the planting and more screening from neighbours' gardens to either side. I also wanted to bring the different parts of the garden together in a more focused design. To make the garden feel larger, I increased the planting areas on either side of the path. Borders were added along the outer edges of the walls in a series of squares and, wishing to complement the natural beauty of the beach rather than try to compete with it, I alternated square panels of planting with blocks of pebbles laid on edge.

Plants had never grown well in

the shallow urn because they were forever drying out and were prone to wind scorch. This problem provided me with a source of inspiration. I had wanted to introduce sculpture somewhere in the garden and, by filling a traditional feature (the urn) with something simple and contemporary (stone balls carved out of pumice), I could play on the juxtaposition of old and new and, in doing so, use the urn to centralize the whole design. Placing pots of clipped box balls along the low walls emphasizes the central axis; the rounded shape is continued with neat, low mounds of *Santolina chamaecyparissus* along the two front boundaries (see above).

Most plants suffer in coastal gardens from harsh wind and sea salt. After nearly two years we are still learning which plants will flourish here and which do not tolerate the difficult conditions.

right

Repeating the globe theme, I placed terracotta pots containing box balls in matching pairs at strategic points. Using box in such an exposed location meant that the plants inevitably suffer wind scorch, especially in their new spring growth, but during the summer this tends to grow out.

<u>left</u>
The simply designed
furniture contributes
much to the view of the
garden from the house;
I like the way the horiz-
ontal and vertical slats
of the table and seats
correspond so well with
the lines of brickwork.

<u>right</u>
The borders in high
summer. The general theme
for the colour palettes
used throughout the garden
is a background of silver-
and grey-foliaged plants,
such as *Santolina chamae-*
cyparissus, lavenders
and *Salvia officinalis*
'Purpurascens', which tone
well with purple. There are
lovely groups of *Bergenia*
cordifolia, Artemisia
'Powis Castle', penstemons
and *Helichrysum petiolare;*
for autumn and winter
effect there is *Sedum*
'Autumn Joy' with *Brachy-*
glottis greyi and various
grasses, such as bluish-
green *Festuca glauca.*

__a broad terrace__
built from old, red stock bricks
opens out from the double doors

__the new beds__
will include a planted
gravel garden

__the central beds__
have planting of year-
round interest, with
penstemon, sedum,
bergenia, artemisia and
helichrysum

__wind-resistant planting__
of evergreen oaks
(*Quercus ilex*), viburnums
and sea buckthorn
(*Hippophae rhamnoides*)

__a young planting__
of large-needled pines
is given temporary
protection by 2m-
(6ft-) high screens
of willow-weave

__the shallow urn__
__on its plinth__
centralizes the whole
garden design

__low woven willow panels__
are placed in the ground
and supported by stout
5 x 2cm (2 x 1in) timber
stakes

__the sea wall boundary__
is edged with mounds
of clipped santolina, protected
by the willow-weave panels

Our plan for the garden included footlights along the central pathway, which would give a low, night-time glow over the terracotta coloured bricks and increase the perceived length of the garden. An uplighter washes the underside of the central vase and stone balls with light, and more uplighters highlight the mature evergreens that grow along one side of the site. These evergreens – oak (*Quercus ilex*), viburnum (*V. tinus*) and sea buckthorn (*Hippophae rhamnoides*) – provide a robust windbreak, protecting the garden from the strong, salt-laden winds. At the base of their trunks are squares of pebbles and sea-washed coarse gravel, designed to create a slightly more intimate and small-scale feeling. On the opposite side, where there is a planting of large-needled pines (*Pinus radiata*), another gravel area is laid along the edge of the lawn. When the budget allows, this is to be a planted gravel garden to balance the bed on the opposite boundary.

The garden is reasonably low maintenance, its only real demands being the cutting of the grass and the trimming of the box balls and santolina mounds. We mulch the beds with crushed sea shells, which is effective in keeping the site relatively free of weeds.

plan & construction

s a n c t u a r y

From time to time we all need to switch off and find a quiet corner where we can take a break
from the pressures of our lives. Although gardens in both town and country are becoming
ever smaller, even the tiniest city yard or roof space can be turned into a sanctuary.
Screening the site and enclosing it with plants will prevent it from being overlooked by
other buildings; the sound of running water adds to the sense of enclosure.

above
A feeling of calm can be
triggered by the simplest
of plants or objects.
This ball of helxine
flourishing in a damp,
sheltered spot exuded
contentment, as if it
would go on thriving and
prospering there for
quite some time.

left
A city, in this case
Paris, seems an
improbable setting for
this garden of rocks,
bamboo and deep shade.
Even in a large garden, a
sanctuary can be created
quite simply by planting a
circle of trees or shrubs
to enclose a small space
containing a seat. Here
you can escape into
another world, even if
only for a few minutes.

Why do people need gardens? It is my firm belief that a
garden can provide us with a sanctuary, offering us a
sense of separation from the outside world. This somewhat
abstract concept finds substantial form in the boundaries
of the garden and the entry point, which might be through
an arch or doorway. Even a space enclosed by buildings
has a certain resonance, for it evokes the walled gardens
of earlier times.

Walled gardens, herb gardens and courtyard gardens
have been places of reflection and meditation over many
centuries and in many cultures. In the Middle Ages
monastic cloister gardens were used to cultivate fruit,
flowers and vegetables, medicinal herbs and rare and
exotic plants. Subsequently, the kitchen garden was
moved away from the main house, where it provided the
best environment for cultivation, and may also have been
a response to the idea that vegetables and fruit were
utilitarian and therefore unattractive.

The garden sanctuary is not only a self-contained place.
In the literature of many cultures it has been used as the
setting for romantic meetings. In tales from the deserts of
the East, an oasis is often described as the venue for a
passionate meeting beside the moonlit water. In the

A very modern and completely uncluttered sanctuary by architect John Pawson, with lovely high trellis walls and a great built-in bench and cut-limestone table at one end. It has a simple balcony treatment with steel cables and a fig-tree balustrade which will look very effective when in leaf.

78 European tradition of courtly love, trysts always took place in a beautiful flower garden.

Despite these literary precedents, I do not think that a sanctuary garden should always be perceived as a lush green environment, bursting with exotic plants. It can be quite the opposite: a minimalist space with very few plants. It can even be as spartan as the garden shown opposite, which contains little more than a seat, water and pebbles. Nothing more is needed to inspire a moment of quiet contemplation.

My own ideal would be a bare space with a single specimen plant, such as a *Brahea armata*, a pyramid *Magnolia grandiflora*, or even a single ball of privet in a fine container. Greening a tiny area, or creating one with perhaps just a few shrubs or trees, is as much of a challenge as organizing space in any other context. I must be honest and admit that I find it much more exciting to make a garden in a small space. I love to transform even the smallest and most unlikely urban niche into a haven and a positive asset.

Tiny gardens seem to have become much more usual in recent years. The crucial thing is that they should still give access to the outside world. If you live in a major city, the

above
There is no better place to lie in a garden than in a hammock. This one is secured by a metal stake at one end which has been disguised by planting.

opposite
In this garden, at a house by the architect Mestre, a stunning water feature has been built into the high boundary wall. The gentle stream of clear water collects on the pebbles, creating a shallow pool.

converted school yard

I must admit that I get more excited these days about creating an oasis in the middle of a city, such as London or New York, than I do about a rural garden. It is much more of a challenge to make a space of this type work when you have obstacles such as high boundaries before you. When I hear people's positive reactions to tiny garden spaces it makes my sense of satisfaction even greater.

The entrance to this garden and flat (a converted classroom) is through a fine stone gateway, with a view of the garden's entire depth. We wanted to retain the view and yet make the space cosy. To achieve this end, the left-hand side was given a thick planting of green-, silver- and purple-leaved shrubs and herbaceous plants.

Grey concrete paving slabs alternate with squares of Cotswold chippings, creating a pattern that recalls the game of hopscotch and the yard's original purpose. Plants such as sedums and *Alchemilla mollis* grow through the gravel, to soften the overall effect.

Uprights on either side of a long, low bench serve as a log store and frame the large window.

garden provides a connection, however slight, with nature and 'the great outdoors'.

I regard tall walls around a small garden as a positive advantage. They give an immediate definition to the space and, being solid, convey a better sense of enclosure than a fence or a hedge. Walls are also a great starting point. You can leave them bare, which is my preference, paint them, or fix a feature to them such as a sundial, or even a water feature (see page 79). They also give a basic framework onto which you can build a structure such as a pergola or a conservatory.

The most obvious use for boundary walls is as a support for plants, either of the self-clinging variety, such as ivies, or those that grow with the aid of wire supports, such as clematis, jasmines or the slightly more tender *Trachelospermum jasminoides*. Pleached or espaliered trees can also create their own interesting framework without taking up too much horizontal space (see page 85).

opposite
On this roof terrace, the silver leaves of an olive tree combine with dark topiary forms to create an effective screen, shutting out the urban rooftop view beyond.

Although I like walls, they are not a prerequisite. You may prefer the challenge of designing a really interesting boundary framework yourself, possibly using the wire mesh shown on page 141 as a support for plants. It is possible to create the effect of high walls by using sections of trellis, an approach which has the immediate advantage that there will be no need for planning permission. Remember that wooden trellis should be treated against rot before it is erected, as this will greatly prolong its life.

If you have a large, open garden, you may feel that you want to create a private space by screening off a small area with plants. If the garden is in a rural setting, you could decide to create a sanctuary garden for yourself by planting a living willow fence around a pool of still water. This combination of water and greenery can convey the lush sense of growth associated with an oasis in the middle of a desert (see page 45). I would certainly include water in my perfect sanctuary garden.

sun-filled haven

left
White canvas awnings
create a sail when open,
and roll back into simple
black box housings fitted
to the main house wall.
Feathery olive trees,
terracotta pots and a low
recliner give the relaxed
atmosphere I was after in
this courtyard garden,
with their associations
of sunny Mediterranean
holidays.

Protected from the buzz of city life by high walls and the L-shaped building, this garden is a tranquil pool of privacy. A central silvery-green planting of olive trees creates an oasis within the space, that has been planted around its boundaries for added shelter. The entire colour palette has been kept to restful shades of cream, grey, silver and blue – a foil to the lovely old red brick walls of the house.

<u>below, from left</u>
■ The dark green-framed conservatory complements the metal windows of the house; tall trees screen the garden from the neighbours.
■ Box balls form a neat border along the wall and disguise the ivy roots.
■ Young pleached limes form the main planting along the side boundary.
■ Ivy underplanted with santolina and box edging just inside the planter.
■ View from the main reception room across the courtyard.

The house, which dates from the early 1900s, has wonderful stone mullion window surrounds and black metal window frames standing out against the red bricks of its walls. The garden is the focus of all the main ground-floor rooms and the conservatory, with three double-arched doorways leading from the main reception room into the garden; to the side are views from the kitchen.

Making the garden feel more enclosed to improve privacy was of prime importance, and planting was to give year-round visual interest, yet be low maintenance. Visual links between house and garden were also important, particularly vistas through the double doors, and the relation of interior and exterior style (the house had just been redesigned and furnished with contemporary furniture and art) was to influence the way forward in the garden design.

For the placing of the garden's central planted feature – the four olive trees – the main axis and views were taken from the central door of the main room. Four square beds were created by taking up

the existing paving and aligning these with the windows. This gave us the central feature, which is already like an inner sanctum within the larger space of the garden. It is tempting to add a water feature there and make it into a symbolic oasis, but for now it makes a perfect semi-private space for alfresco dining.

Old magnolia trees with sparse foliage along the boundary were replaced with seven pleached lime trees. Once mature, these will be kept at a height for maximum privacy and will contribute the desired graphic or linear quality, in keeping with the clean lines of the house and other planting. Behind these, the walls are clad in ivy which provides interest during the months when the limes are bare. Underplanting the limes are square blocks of *Santolina incana*, catmint (*Nepeta* sp.) and various herbs used in the kitchen.

Designed to link with the stone window surrounds, the raised-bed planter, which forms a right-angle along two boundary walls, was rendered and then left with a natural finish. A reconstituted stone coping was added along its length, wide enough to sit on, to provide additional seating when this is needed.

below
When redesigning the garden, all the walls of the L-shaped planter were rendered to cover up the brickwork. The top was given a wide coping of reconstituted stone, which has a strong visual effect. It forms a bench along two sides of the garden, as well as an ideal resting place for cups and glasses.

left
The four olive trees form a small, secluded square within the wide paved area of the garden, and at the same time the individual trees are perfectly aligned along vistas from the house. Olives were chosen for their feathered quality, and the fact that they move in the breeze and catch the light; ever-greens or pleached trees here would have been too rigid and formal in their effect. The square boxwood underplantings give the scheme its necessary structure.

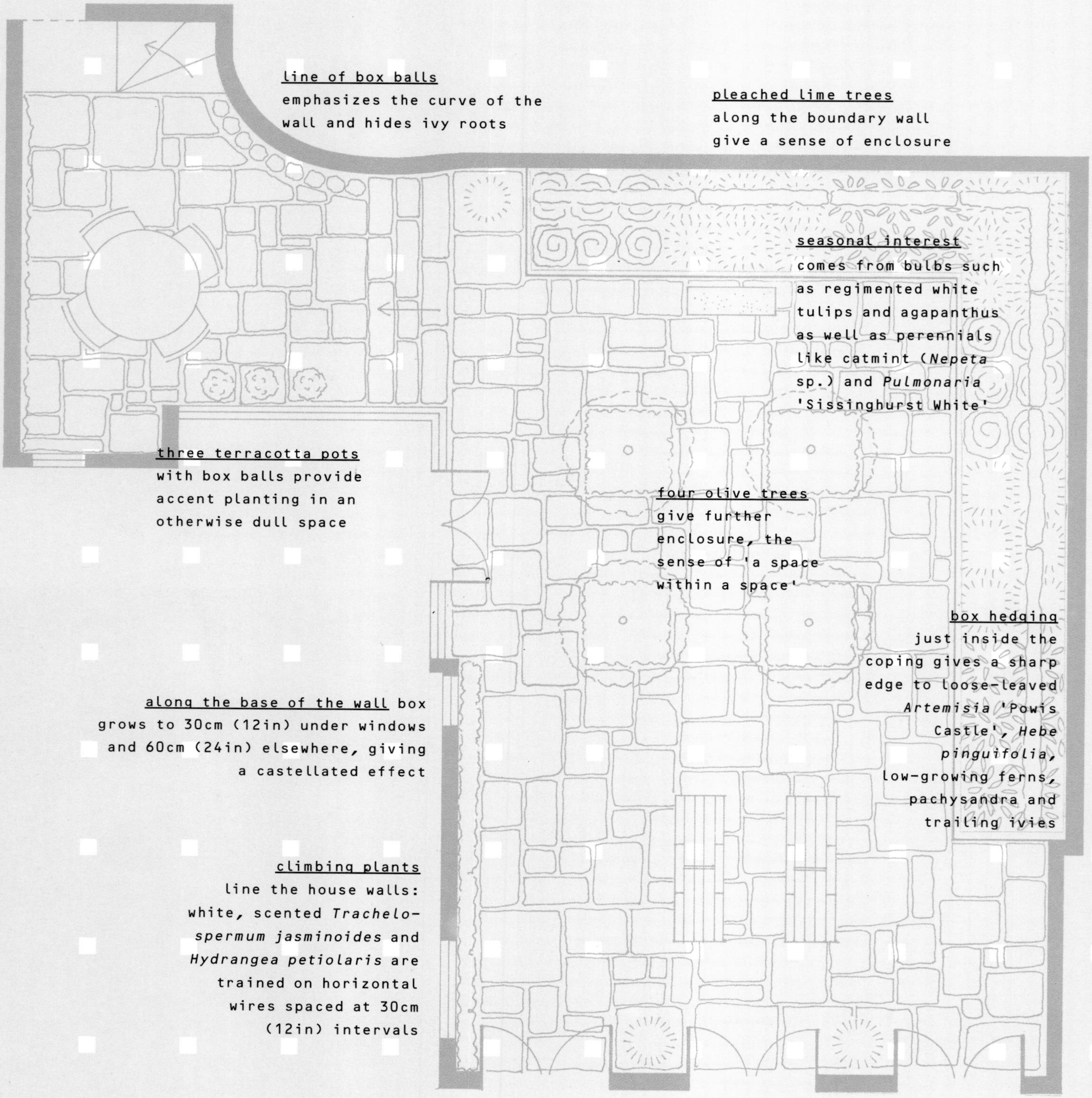

line of box balls
emphasizes the curve of the
wall and hides ivy roots

pleached lime trees
along the boundary wall
give a sense of enclosure

seasonal interest
comes from bulbs such
as regimented white
tulips and agapanthus
as well as perennials
like catmint (*Nepeta*
sp.) and *Pulmonaria*
'Sissinghurst White'

88

three terracotta pots
with box balls provide
accent planting in an
otherwise dull space

four olive trees
give further
enclosure, the
sense of 'a space
within a space'

box hedging
just inside the
coping gives a sharp
edge to loose-leaved
Artemisia 'Powis
Castle', *Hebe
pinguifolia*,
low-growing ferns,
pachysandra and
trailing ivies

along the base of the wall box
grows to 30cm (12in) under windows
and 60cm (24in) elsewhere, giving
a castellated effect

climbing plants
line the house walls:
white, scented *Trachelo-
spermum jasminoides* and
Hydrangea petiolaris are
trained on horizontal
wires spaced at 30cm
(12in) intervals

The garden was designed around the soft, warm tones of York stone paving, honey-coloured timber and shrubby, feathery plants associated with Mediterranean sun – particularly olives, santolina and herbs such as thyme and rosemary. The slatted seats and recliners link in colour with the warm wood flooring inside the house; the simple and elegant furnishings echo those inside. The garden flows nicely into the ground floor reception when all three sets of doors are open. The garden was designed to be as low maintenance as possible. The box requires clipping once or twice a year to keep its shape, as do the pleached limes to thicken them up. The olives, being slow-growing, barely need clipping. An automatic watering system was installed for the planters, its tap hidden beneath a loose paving slab marked with an X.

At night, uplighters cast dappled light up through the branches of the four olive trees and highlight the pleached limes in the boundary beds.

plan & construction

minimal

As a garden design concept, 'minimalism' has every reason to be popular. The minimalist garden is built around one or two simple ideas or objects: one good piece of sculpture or a water feature would suffice. Plant varieties and colour palette will be restricted to a few carefully selected specimen or feature plants. The garden that emerges from this treatment will be both cost effective and low maintenance. Keep the chemistry simple — that's what it's all about.

above
A roof garden high above New York City by Jeff Mendoza. The boundary wall of bamboo poles echoes the vertical lines of the buildings behind, while the rocks, gravel and clipped evergreens offer a striking contrast.

left
A tranquil atmosphere has been created in the garden of the Glass House, in London, by architects Future Systems through the use of glass, metal, rendered white walls and well-placed rocks set in a wave of grass. The curved copper screen hides the rear gate. Using the same tiled flooring inside and out helps the garden flow into the house.

Many contemporary garden designers work closely with architects or at least make use of modern architectural materials. Consequently, they have developed a streamlined approach, using simple lines and an uncluttered palette. To some extent, minimalism was the inevitable outcome of this new development. A minimalist style may have a reputation for being rather severe, or even bleak, but this need not be the case – it can just as well be warm and playful (see pages 16–17, 94). And it's not essential to use only high-tech materials; you can still get a contemporary feel from grasses or one or two plants. A traditional material such as York stone or slate can be updated with clean-cut surfaces and edges. York stone is not dissimilar to cut limestone, which is one of my favourite materials (see page 92). I use limestone not only for paving but also to edge or face planters and as an inlay between slightly darker cut York stone, which makes an interesting contrast, almost like a border around a terrace.

When I design a garden that is to have a mildly minimal feel, I always begin by considering the colour palette. Colour may well determine my choice of hard materials, which will also directly relate to the type and style of planting. If I am using a natural material, such as a beige-

geometry in stone

This is one of my favourite gardens because its effect is clean and simple, but it successfully mixes different paving materials. It was designed to echo the simple, clean lines of the interior of the house, like a piece of modern sculpture adjacent to it. It is visually exciting, but has a sense of calm that makes it feel peaceful and relaxing.

Limestone is the chief hard material in the garden, used for the wavy path, the long perimeter bench and the coping to the balustraded wall. As a contrast to the curved path, we laid 60cm- (24in-) square grey paving stones in a regular pattern, which I felt would work nicely against the softness of the limestone and the lawn's edge.

The tubular balustrading was painted to colour-match the house, and is set off against a backdrop of high willow-weave boundary fence in a natural, dark reddish colour. The main planting along the right-hand side of the garden is in a 1.2m- (4ft-) deep planter. A second area of planting was placed (by permission) in the communal area at the end of the garden; we planted mostly ever-greens here to create a year-round screen.

The hard landscaping was punctuated with plain stone pots containing specimen trees such as *Cedrus deodora* and *Acer palmatum* Atropurpureum Group.

<u>above</u>
A crisply angular polished
black marble surround to
a raised lawn contrasts
with dark evergreen
planting at Parc André
Citroen, Paris.

coloured stone, I may well choose a hardwood to go with
it, such as Iroko for decking. The wood will be treated with
oil, so that it doesn't weather too much and stays honey-
coloured rather than turning silver-grey. These materials
also go well with lawn, formal pools or areas of gravel. For
freestanding containers I choose an appropriate style of
pot or urn in a simple shape, which may be made up in
reconstituted Cotswold stone, and combines well with the
other shades and textures. A warmer-toned alternative
would be a lime-washed terracotta pot. By planting it with
a very structural type of tree, such as *Acer palmatum* var.
dissectum, where the foliage gives a layered effect (not
dissimilar to a cedar of Lebanon), you obtain a strongly
sculptural form, the outline contributing much to the clean,
graphic lines of decking or paving.

Built-in seating is an excellent choice for a minimalist
look – cushions and ornate furniture shapes would be too
cluttered and distracting. If the garden is to have one or
more raised beds, I suggest that their edges are made
wide enough to sit on; this is useful if you need extra space
for people when entertaining. Outlining the raised beds
with wide edgings also strengthens them as features,
which in turn focuses attention on the plants within them.

far left
Gravel squares set into the grass lead the eye past the house to the swimming pool beyond.

left
Three perfectly spherical stone balls create a focal point on a sloping expanse of lawn.

right
A single bold but graceful plant lends atmosphere to this gleaming courtyard, which makes a striking contrast to the softly verdant landscape garden with its tall trees glimpsed beyond.

In a minimal garden you will keep to a quite rigid design, but you do have the option of changing its pace. For example, a change of level could be introduced, or contrasting surface materials may be used. A stairway incorporating a water feature was one of the best examples I have seen of making the most of a change of level (see page 166). Well-designed steps, their risers made of limestone and the treads of turf, were placed on either side of a stepped rill. This was wide enough to allow a good flow of water to circulate and, though simple, formed a delightful water feature with small pools at top and bottom.

The concept of minimal gardens is nothing new in the Far East, as some of the oldest Japanese gardens demonstrate. I often follow the same principles, perhaps using an attractive stone feature set within a gravel area, or laying out paths or bridges as a series of left and right angles to confuse and ward off evil spirits. I learned of this practice from the designers of Zen gardens and I have also seen it recommended by Feng Shui experts.

I prefer to use groups of single-species plantings, such as acers, flowering cherries (*Prunus subhirtella autumnalis* or *P. laurocerasus* 'Otto Luyken'), or grasses (best of all are *Miscanthus sinensis* and *Festuca glauca*), or a bamboo such as *Phyllostachys variegata*. I use some plants as ground cover – ivies, pachysandra and hostas – and some as feature plants, especially *Mahonia japonica* and bamboos, some of which grow to 6m (20ft) tall. (Bamboo can be very invasive, so take care with its siting.)

above

Here, in one of London's finest squares, opposite the Hempel Hotel, is an example of minimal design at its best. The clarity of positioning of every plant and the attention to the smallest of details takes your breath away.

In a minimal garden you may select just one specimen plant of outstanding beauty, as the hard landscaping components will say everything else for you. You may wish to have topiary as your specimen plant: for example, the airy forms of a 'cloud' yew tree might be appealing. Alternatively, you could select something even less formal, such as a feathery olive tree.

I am always struck by how well the concept 'less is more' relates to gardening. I would far rather design a garden with five plant varieties than one with fifty or even a

<u>left</u>
The clean lines of the stone walls rise dramatically out of perfectly still water.

<u>below</u>
These rocks and the raked gravel around them are part of a Japanese garden. The designers of minimal- ist gardens have always drawn inspiration from Japanese design philosophy.

hundred. With a minimal plant selection, each variety must have the capacity to add its own special quality to the project. Obviously, a block planting may be repeated over and over again. If you were to take a block of five varieties, it could be repeated to form a stronger pattern of ten blocks which would build up into a bold statement.

When planning the planting for a minimal garden you might be well advised to select only varieties with white flowers. These will imbue your design with a freshness and clarity of effect. The colours of the hard landscaping are

also important. Walls should be rendered in a natural colour or painted white to maximize the light – an especially important consideration in northerly latitudes like the British Isles, Canada and the northern states of the US.

A designer working with much better light, perhaps in Australia, California or parts of the Mediterranean, could afford to be more adventurous about the colour of the garden boundaries. It might even be feasible to paint whole walls in a strong colour (see page 49) without in any way diminishing the available light in the garden.

cool symmetry

cool symmetry

Here I was handed the most perfect opportunity for a minimal garden treatment – an almost blank canvas on which to work. The house faces onto a small, rectangular site with a high, blank, ivy-clad wall at the end, forming an ideal backdrop for a symmetrical design and a stunning water feature.

left
A striking piece of theatrical minimalism in the form of a water feature takes the eye up to a dramatically planted backdrop: the end wall of an adjacent building, disguised by ivy.

A high end wall, side boundaries some 2m (6ft) tall and trees to either side make this small back garden a shady site, but the height of the boundaries did mean that the garden was completely enclosed and private.

The client and I shared the belief that there should be a strong link between the interior and exterior spaces, so this was a particularly good project for us. The interior of the house is simple, with wooden floors in natural or white-painted timber. The furniture, covered in white ticking, has clean lines and an air of comfort.

The well-designed interior lighting creates different effects, which may alter the mood or highlight certain features. In designing the garden, the graphic simplicity of the house exterior and interior was kept in mind.

The client didn't want to lose the dark green ivy covering the rear wall and the fairly mature bamboo just inside it, and he wanted to keep two trees – a mature, double, pink-flowering cherry tree on the plot's left-hand side and a gingko to the right. Otherwise we were given a free hand with the scheme.

At one of our first meetings, we

from left
■ White impatiens by the terrace makes a light-show against cool rendered walls.
■ Clipped box set off by clean limestone paving.
■ A custom-designed light box with a sandblasted glass panel.

suggested placing a central water feature near the rear wall, as this would help with the symmetrical layout we felt the garden demanded. Early on we decided that the rectangular, upright form of the water feature should make a central focal point, just in front of the rear boundary. This feature was built of blockwork, rendered and painted white in order to give the cleanest possible look to this end of the garden.

To bring scale to the rear wall and make it less intimidating, we decided to build a 2m- (6ft-) high secondary wall just inside it. This would form a continuous line with the side walls and would also hide the bare ivy roots. This wall, which matched the height of the water feature exactly, was also rendered and painted.

The water feature with its built-in pool of water has a low surround, wide enough to form a bench; its top was clad in Iroko. Two free-standing Iroko benches situated between square galvanized containers were custom-built for the walls on either side. At the house end is a raised terrace, also in Iroko, the timber features at either end making for a nice

balance in the garden. Matching wide wooden steps lead down from the terrace on either side of the central paved steps; these contain storage space for small items of equipment, like hand tools.

To link in with the water feature and terrace, we used a soft approach to the hard landscaping, laying two symmetrical areas of cream-coloured limestone paving, with a connecting central path leading to the water feature. The limestone path is divided by a long, narrow, planted rill. This was originally designed to contain low-growing ornamental grass, but it looked too unstructured, and was exchanged for castellated box-wood (*Buxus sempervirens*), which has the necessary impact to lead the eye to the straight white wall of the fountain. This whiteness is echoed by twin panels of white gravel, laid to either side of the path.

Along the side walls are slightly raised planted areas with surrounding edgings made of folding soft zinc (galvanized iron would achieve almost the same effect). They contain mainly small-leaved bamboos underplanted with solid ground cover of plain green ivy

below
Custom-made wall lights also serve as a shelf for white-flowered stocks in matching galvanized pots.

left
The starkly minimal form of the pool and fountain and the lines of paving leading to it give the courtyard a sanctuary-like feel, emphasized by the overhead planting. The water feature stands at the far end of the garden, on an axis leading from the glazed double doors at the back of the house.

The construction of the
water feature is decept-
ively simple: it is built
of blockwork and then
rendered, with a painted
finish. A sandblasted
glass panel is positioned
in front of the blockwork,
standing in the nickel-
plated trough which forms
the reservoir of water.
An uplighter behind the
glass illuminates the
water cascading down the
polished glass section.

Plastic furniture achieved
the right transparent feel
at the other end of the
garden from the water
feature.

and pachysandra: an all-year-round evergreen mixture. To counterbalance and soften the harsh lines of the water feature, we placed to either side of it a 90cm-(3ft-) square container, made of plastic but painted cream; this pair of planters contains topiarized yew 'cloud' trees, underplanted with ivy.

Each of the four tall galvanized pots is planted with a boxwood cube of the same dimensions as the pot itself, to link with the castellated box down the middle of the central path. Two further 90cm- (3ft-) square containers complete the symmetry, standing at the end of each bamboo border and butting up to the terrace of decking. These pots are planted with spiral-shaped yew trees and underplanted with seasonal flowers, all in white: bulbs for the spring, busy lizzies (*Impatiens*) in summer, and heathers in winter.

At night, the garden receives dramatic treatment, the water feature and its lighting being the most striking part of the whole scene: underwater lights behind the sandblasted glass in the water feature cast a rippling, dance-like effect over the water's surface. Fittings in the risers of the terrace steps throw light across the gravel panels in the central path at night, while the four trees in their large planters are dramatized by uplighting, from lights in the planters themselves. The same effect is given to the bamboos in the side beds, where a couple of fittings in each bed throw a dappled wash of light up through their leaves. For the side walls of the house, outside the conservatory, I designed a pair of rectangular wall lights to throw out just a little light over the decking; these also act as a shelf upon which to place a row of three galvanized pots filled with white-flowered seasonal plants. In the wall to each side of the terrace, I also positioned two brick lights with filtered covers which cast a pleasant glow across the decking.

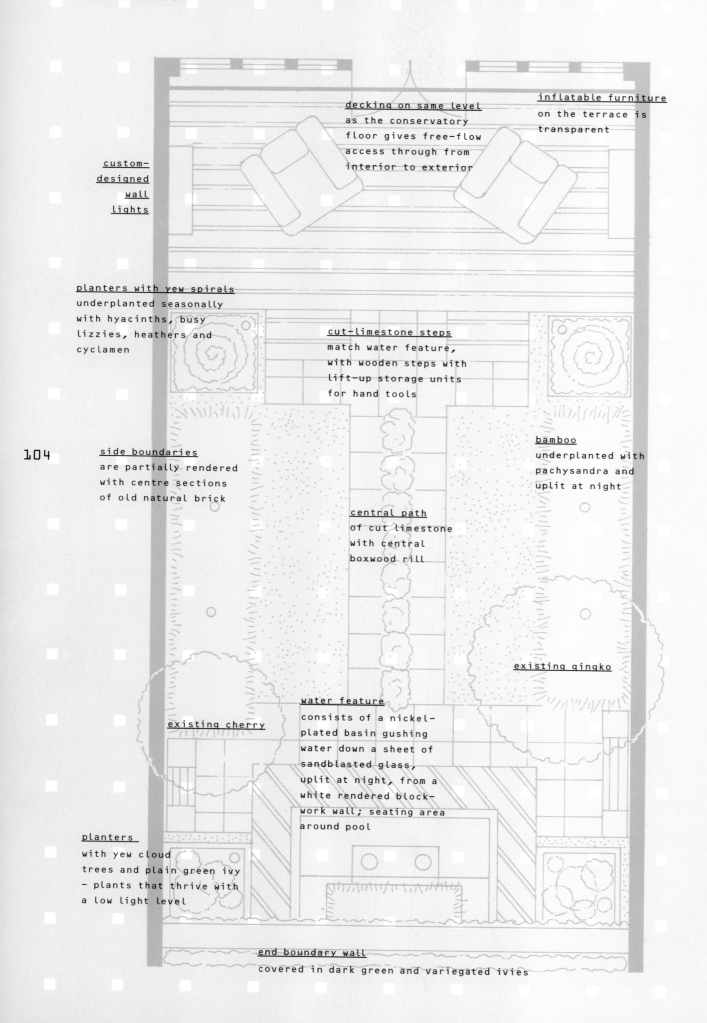

decking on same level
as the conservatory
floor gives free-flow
access through from
interior to exterior

inflatable furniture
on the terrace is
transparent

custom-
designed
wall
lights

planters with yew spirals
underplanted seasonally
with hyacinths, busy
lizzies, heathers and
cyclamen

cut-limestone steps
match water feature,
with wooden steps with
lift-up storage units
for hand tools

104

side boundaries
are partially rendered
with centre sections
of old natural brick

bamboo
underplanted with
pachysandra and
uplit at night

central path
of cut limestone
with central
boxwood rill

existing gingko

water feature
consists of a nickel-
plated basin gushing
water down a sheet of
sandblasted glass,
uplit at night, from a
white rendered block-
work wall; seating area
around pool

existing cherry

planters
with yew cloud
trees and plain green ivy
- plants that thrive with
a low light level

end boundary wall
covered in dark green and variegated ivies

The perspective we chose for this garden, a symmetrical vista to the water feature, makes it feel quite large. We wanted to continue this spacious feel by leaving the terrace as clear of furnishings as possible, and transparent plastic inflatable chairs seemed the best solution.

To make use of the terrace at all times, we fitted a white awning to the rear wall of the house, raised up above the conservatory, which is the same length and width as the decking. It is automatically controlled from inside the house. When fully out, it provides protection from the midday sun and the occasional shower of rain that falls on balmy summer nights.

Vacuuming is a major part of this garden's maintenance, as any leaf on the limestone or gravel completely spoils its ultra-clean look. Otherwise maintenance is restricted to clipping the shaped evergreens and keeping the bamboos under control. The containers require a seasonal change of plants every so often. The garden is fitted with an automatic watering system, so its irrigation needs more or less look after themselves.

plan & construction

sensory experience

Your garden should be a sensuous place, imbued with the power to transport you to another world, where you are free to follow your thoughts to their limit and to be released from everyday pressures. When designing your garden, concentrate on each of the five senses in turn, so that you can bring added depth to this aspect of the garden.

above

The glimpses of water seen through the uprights of this pergola lend a magical atmosphere to the land-scape beyond.

opposite

This amazing, sculpted tree stands in a sea of brightly coloured dahlias. Small pipes arranged among the branches support artificial flowers. Water dripping from each pipe forms tiny cascades, creating the impression of gentle rain. This is a wonderful example of moving art within the garden.

The paradise garden is my starting point for thinking about the sensual dimension of a design. I use this term to encompass Adam and Eve's Eden and the paradise garden described in the Koran. The Islamic faithful are promised eternal bliss in a garden of 'spreading shade', 'fruits, fountains and pomegranates' and 'cool pavilions'. In both traditions, the gardens are bound up with the sumptuous delights of flowers, scents, fruits and birdsong. They are places where mankind is in harmony with nature and all five senses may find satisfaction.

Water was certainly central to the Persians' idea of the paradise garden. Just to watch its gentle ripples or the sparkling light on a pond is pleasure enough, but the sound of gently flowing or bubbling water adds another whole dimension to the garden.

It is not difficult today, even in a small garden, to do just as those Mogul garden designers did and introduce a small canal or rill. This can simply be a narrow water-filled channel running through the middle of a site. If space permits, there could be a cross-axis at the halfway point, with pools of water set at a slightly lower level to either side of the main channel. The water usually flows from one end to either the midpoint or the far end of the channel,

right
Japanese wind chimes add
a layer of sound to the
garden, bringing a sense
of the exotic to its atmosphere. This is a very
positive addition to any
Feng Shui garden.

far left
The water running over the
mesh walls of this enclosure looks good with the
silver-grey of willow
(Salix exigua).

left
The trunk of a silver birch
reflected in the shallow
pool is echoed by a clear
perspex column rising out
of the water, creating a
link between natural and
man-made.

108 where it will need to be recirculated via a pump. If you happen to have slightly sloping ground, you could design your water feature to flow over very shallow steps, which would generate a slightly stronger sound (see pages 166 and 167). A more vigorous flow of water will serve the dual purpose of disguising the sounds of the real world beyond the garden boundary.

Even on a small balcony or roof terrace there is no excuse for an absence of water. It can be simply introduced as a wall fountain with a self-contained pump. There need not even be a large amount of water: just the lightest, constantly flowing trickle creates a soothing atmosphere. In some Japanese-style water features, the water drips into a piece of hollowed-out bamboo set on a pivot. When the bamboo is full it tips forwards, allowing the water to flow into a basin or pool, and in so doing taps a stone before returning to be refilled and repeat the process. I find that the sound of water dripping as the bamboo fills, then the gentle rushing followed by a quick tap is a very satisfying, sensuous experience.

The 1998 theme for the Chaumont Garden Festival in France was 'water' and ideas there ranged from water gardens with wild reeds to the atmospheric gauzy funnels seen on page 35 and the circular enclosure shown above left. When you stand inside this structure you are entirely enclosed by the water that flows down the mesh wall. The experience is both soothing and cooling on a hot day. Otherwise, water bubbling up through a metal or glass column and falling back down into a shallow pool is not difficult to install. It could flow over a couple of steps or even fall as a single drop, like a miniature waterfall.

Any discussion of water would not be complete without a reference to the idea of an outdoor shower or an alfresco hot-tub. To use either of these in the garden is a powerfully sensual experience.

If the garden permits it, a swimming pool is of course the ultimate sensory experience. Nowadays a pool can play a pivotal role in the design of a garden that is large enough to accommodate one. Its siting is an important decision, as it should create a positive visual experience

rather than jarring with its surroundings. This is why I cannot abide pools that are lined with blue tiles. I always line
mine – swimming pool or garden pond – in black or dark
green. Both colours guarantee wonderful reflections in the
water. If you do choose a dark colour for your swimming
pool, white safety lines should be painted on the steps.

The swimming pool should relate to the design of the
garden and to the position of the house. Ideally it should
be sited close to the main house and your outdoor entertaining area, otherwise, you may find that you have to build
separate changing-room facilities. I always maintain that
you need a fridge near a pool area; I don't think you can
have one without the other. After all, having a cool drink by
the pool on a warm summer's day is another of life's
sensory pleasures!

Should it be quite impossible to bring water into the
garden, there are ways of introducing a watery theme or
feeling to the site. Drifts of planting can be combined with
carefully arranged pebbles, to suggest a dry river bed

sensory roof garden

The many different textures of
greens and greys, the highly
polished glass fibre containers
and the beautiful pebbles laid on
edge make this roof garden a very
sensuous place.

The pebbles complement the
limestone paving running from the
interior of the house and onto the
roof. The planting design is all
about leaf shapes and texture.
It includes *Choisya ternata*, the
textured leaves of the fig, the ovate
form of the pittosporum and the
Japanese mock orange, planted
for its heavenly scent. The scent
of the mock orange marries well
with that of the jasmine growing
against the house. Terracotta pots
planted with thyme, lavender and
rosemary lend softness to the
scheme. The pungent scents of the
aromatic herbs mingle with the
other fragrances to add another
sensuous dimension to the
garden's atmosphere.

left
This pleasing, curved bed
is kept free of gravel by
a fine metal trim. The two
metal curves meet in a
satisfying acute angle,
creating an organic flow
which affords great visual
satisfaction.

where water once flowed (see pages 64, 114). You can achieve a wonderfully watery feel using certain types of foliage such as blue fescue grasses, *Eryngium* thistles and lovely drifts of silver and grey foliage plants like *Santolina*, *Senecio*, *Artemisia* and the late-summer blue-flowered shrub *Caryopteris clandonensis* cultivars.

Scent is an exciting aspect of the sensory experience. It's always nice to surprise people strolling in the garden with an unexpected fragrance, a sudden waft of something delicious. There is nothing better than a late summer's evening with those wonderful drifts of distinctive fragrance from flowers which release their perfumes at night in order to attract moths. Datura, known as angel's trumpets (*Brugmansia*), has yellow, perfectly formed pendant flowers which mix wonderfully with the superb evergreen climber *Trachelospermum jasminoides*, and its delightful clusters of white flowers. This plant always reminds me of a house in Majorca where I planted all the walls with summer jasmine, with its scented, similar-shaped small white flowers.

 113

<u>above</u>
Warm-coloured wood provides a sympathetic path through the tall grasses swaying in the wind.

<u>above left</u>
A gauzy, translucent screen lends a touch of the exotic as it protects a young tree.

<u>left</u>
This garden engages the senses fully with rich colours, varied textures, scented and aromatic plants, and hard-landscaping materials. The clean lines of brick, concrete and galvanized metal create an air of calm to offset the busy planting within the raised beds.

canal reflections

<u>above</u>
The shallow hump-backed
bridge takes its shape from
traditional stone canal
bridges. A bed of pebbles
has been laid in a
waterless channel beneath
the bridge to create the
effect of a dry creek.

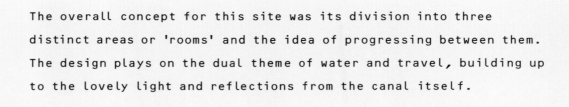

The overall concept for this site was its division into three distinct areas or 'rooms' and the idea of progressing between them. The design plays on the dual theme of water and travel, building up to the lovely light and reflections from the canal itself.

<u>below, from left</u>
- Detail of dry river bed with drifts of pebbles.
- Plants twine along the canal-side rope boundary.
- A terracotta figurine nestles in the shade of plants.
- Machine-cut and drilled York stone water feature: water bubbles up out of each piece of cut stone.

Water, whether in the form of river, stream, canal or the sea itself, is always a source of inspiration and this garden benefits enormously from its site beside the canal.

Our client wanted to build a conservatory on the site of the sunken garden at the back of his house. This also provided an opportunity for redesigning the garden, which had originally been planted in the late 1960s.

The first of the three 'room' divisions was a paved kitchen-dining area at the back of the house. In order to make space for the conservatory, we had to push the lower level of the garden back towards the canal. This gave us the space to build a barbecue into the kitchen area and to introduce a larger table in a sitting area reminiscent of a canal boat.

A miniature hump-backed bridge, like an old-fashioned stone bridge over a canal, linked the first two rooms of the garden together. The bridge crosses a dry creek formed from large and small rounded pebbles. This brings the theme of water into the heart of the garden. I originally planned to make the bridge from stone, but after much thought I chose timber

left
The wonderfully sinuous
form of the corkscrew
hazel (*Corylus avellana*
'Contorta').

for its ability to bring a feeling of
warmth and softness to the
garden, creating a contrast with
the hard surfaces of the paved
area. The curved shape of the
bridge is also reminiscent of the
curved tunnels that are common
to waterways throughout England.

Beyond the bridge is the lawn
and planted area – the second
garden room. Water spouts from
a water feature made from three
hollowed-out pieces of cut York
stone which matches the stone
used around the seating area.

Beyond the lawn lies the third
room, the deck by the canal. The
deck itself is designed to convey
the sensation of being on a
moored boat.

All the materials for the garden
had to arrive on site by way of the
canal, which provided the perfect
excuse to rebuild the landing

stage. And as the client didn't
want a garden shed or any other
outbuildings, we also built in some
dry-storage units.

The landing stage was enlarged
without losing any space in the
garden. This was achieved by
extending the area out over the
water. The extended landing stage
provides a lovely place to sit and
eat or just enjoy the view. A ladder
built into the design gives access
to a boat moored below. When
not in use, the boat is locked in an
upright position above the deck as
a security measure.

The new rear boundary became
part of the structure, taking the
form of a series of built-in
planters and a line of timber posts
linked together with natural coir
rope. The rope was introduced
to tie in with the nautical theme
of the site.

above
When I first saw this
garden it looked typical
of a medium-sized town
plot: a long, narrow strip
of land that normally leads
nowhere. But in this
instance there was a sur-
prise at the far end – a
lovely canal with adjacent
tree-lined gardens and an
attractive brick school
building beyond the tow-
path on the opposite bank.

left
The raised wooden deck
enjoys views over the
canal and back to the
garden, making it an ideal
sitting area. The tall water
feature can be seen in
the foreground.

118

The planting in the garden is mostly in lines and drifts designed to represent flowing water. The plants have been chosen to look good with the timber and stones of the hard landscaping. Tactile, spiky-textured plants bring a sense of exotic, far-flung places, a sensation reinforced by features such as a little red clay figurine and some oriental wind chimes.

We retained the more structural plants from the original planting and added a good selection of evergreens, focusing on plants native to coastal areas. Softer, herbaceous planting was used to break up the structured appearance of the evergreens. We tried at the same time to bring a slightly oriental theme to the area by using grasses, bamboos and tree peonies.

Pots of seasonal colour are positioned near to the house, and indoor plants are also planted in pots in the conservatory, creating a strong link between the inside and outside living spaces. Planters on the dockside contain evergreen shrubs like *Fatsia japonica* as well as small-leaved bamboos (*Phyllostachys* sp.) and *Phormium tenax*.

Around the area that would be used to entertain guests we feature-lit various plants. This is a technique which can be used to give the garden a feeling of greater depth. The deck area is always lit at night for reasons of security and safety.

opposite
Seen from the towpath,
the deck and garden are
at an elevated level.
Mature trees partially
screen the house from
the water.

realization

the timber deck
stands out over the
water, supported by steel
joists. It houses built-
in storage and a ladder

timber planters
link with the theme of
wood used throughout the
design. They also lend
the garden extra height,
stopping it from being
dimished by the size of
the surrounding trees

the drilled York stone
water feature has a
reservoir pool beneath,
covered by pebbles

the central area of soft
landscaping,
with lawn and planting,
contrasts with the hard-
landscape structures at
both ends of the garden

boundary wall shared with
neighbours removed for
added feeling of space

cut York stone-clad
retaining walls give a
sparkling clean finish
with a granite-topped
table

a built-in barbecue
with a large stone
top acts as a work
surface

built-in seating
in slatted timber
makes good use of
the supporting walls

a conservatory
creates the perfect link
between house and garden

rough York
stone terrace
with plain
reconstituted
pots for a
decorative touch

At the same time as we were asked to redesign the garden, our client was adding a conservatory to the rear of the property at basement level. This meant that the already sunken garden needed to be excavated further to accommodate a good-sized terrace for entertaining.

The decision was taken to pave the conservatory and the area nearest the house with irregular-sized slabs of York stone. With the terrace and conservatory at the same ground level, this gives a strong contemporary feel, with one material flowing from inside to outside. On one side of the terrace is a work surface with a built-in barbecue. Opposite, a built-in bench along two sides also serves as a retaining wall. It teams with the paving as its surface is composed of squares of cut York stone, and the same material is used for the steps leading up to the lawn and the planted area of the garden.

Near to the decking, three squared columns are grouped together to form a water feature. Cut from York stone – which links them to the terrace and the built-in bench – the columns give a contemporary feel. The tallest has been drilled through the middle to allow water to spout from its top over all four sides, water being pumped from a reservoir underneath. The top of the column and the mechanics of the feature are disguised under a wire mesh grille, covered in pebbles.

Everything had to be delivered or removed from the bottom of the garden via a barge, as this was easier than taking materials through the house.

plan & construction

inside out

Contemporary garden designers often seek to disguise or at least diminish the boundaries between the house and garden by making a deliberate link between features of the interior and exterior designs. Modern houses, restaurants and offices, with their great expanses of glass windows and doors, are ideally suited to this treatment, while the greening of roofs and balconies is a space-gaining extension of the same idea.

As a designer, I see improving the link between the interior and the exterior as the key to creating a good contemporary garden. How the garden is viewed from the house is of vital importance, and by getting this right you create the foundation for a firm relationship between the interior and exterior spaces: what I call dissolving walls.

Creating a frame through which the garden may be seen from indoors is of particular relevance in a modern house with large windows and a small garden. Even the rooms on the higher floors of a building can have their own garden view. If the natural view is unappealing, it can always be disguised or softened by greenery.

A neglected, partly covered or awkward outdoor space adjacent to the house can sometimes be turned into an extension of the interior space instead. One obvious way of achieving this is to add a conservatory onto your house. Whether it is used as a greenhouse, a dining room, a place to relax or even a gymnasium, it will be a valuable adddition to your property.

An indoor–outdoor area does not necessarily have to be a living space. It could be a light-well or a walkway that needs to be brought alive with some simple but striking planting, as seen in the small courtyard above.

left
The clean lines of this room with its glass walls give a perfect, uninterrupted view through to the woodland. Tall columns on the left seem to emulate the vertical trunks of the trees. The simple potted fig tree completes the link with the natural world outside.

right
Large glass windows or doors make the connection between inside and out; the clever use of materials, lighting and furnishings exploit it further, drawing the eye through in a very direct way.

below right
Giant pots make an intriguing play with scale; planted up, they provide a warm outdoor dining arbour.

Nowadays the whole outside wall of a house can be made of glass. Such a feature will be even more effective if the glass is double height, reaching mezzanine or first floor level, giving a garden view to a greater number of rooms. The glass window of the house on the left drops below ground level, giving natural light to a previously dark basement, so that the garden contributes to the look of the whole interior.

By using French windows or glass walling, the style of the interior can be continued out to a terrace or courtyard outside. This link is easy to achieve using modern flooring materials; it is even better when there are wide-opening or sliding doors which allow a total flow. In some contemporary buildings, metal and reinforced glass floors are used for inside and out: the courtyard garden on page 90 uses metal plate flooring either side of the exterior glass wall. The same link can be achieved with a timber floor (see page 23) although timber is not so easy to match, and you have to remember that exterior wood will weather with age, however it's treated. Alternatives would be to use slate or tiles for both interior and exterior, but matting or carpet can also be linked visually, by using similar-coloured stone, concrete slabs or even an area of white or coloured

right

Long rills either side of the walkway around this house in Australia reflect the architecture and add a thrilling dimension to the garden.

right

The use of glass walls makes the pool outside this house appears as an extension of the living room.

left

Huge glass doors glide open over a liquid pool of reflection – in fact bronze-coloured metal flooring. The space taken up by large glass doors like these gives the feeling that the garden is flowing into the house. Here, lovely white climbers predominate, such as the deliciously scented *Trachelospermum jasminoides*, softening the line of the door frame.

gravel outside. My most successful inside–outside gardens are those where I have taken the glass of a conservatory or rear window right down to a smooth, cut limestone floor, laid in a continuous paved pattern from the house through the conservatory and across the width of the garden terrace. For a sense of continuity, rendered walls around an outside terrace can always be painted a similar colour to those inside.

I like to use planting to reinforce the visual link made by the hard surfaces. You can achieve this by using plants of similar habits inside and outside. In a small space I might use a spiky cactus inside and a cordyline or phormium outside. I reinforce the link by using the same style of container inside and out. To take the theme further, I might run a raised shelf holding planted pots along the interior and exterior walls. One such shelf was constructed about 2 metres (6 feet) high along a solid side wall inside a conservatory; the shelf continued at the same height around a walled exterior courtyard. This kind of device works even better if both shelves are made of the same material, such as galvanized metal. I placed domes of helxine (*Soleirolia soleirolii*, commonly called 'mind your own business'), along the inside shelf in small, circular,

above
Christopher Bradley-Hole's
award-winning garden
design for the 1998 Chelsea
Flower Show transcends
the space within and gives
vistas onto the planting.

galvanized pots; outside were similar, larger pots planted with clipped boxwood domes (*Buxus sempervirens*). Using galvanized pots gives a fresh look, though terracotta would do just as well; the planting can of course be changed seasonally. You can do the same on a larger scale, using galvanized tanks for containers in a conservatory and repeating them in the garden. Choosing plants that have a similar habit and appearance gives the effect of a mirror image through the glass.

Where glass house or conservatory walls are not appropriate, other links can be introduced to keep the inside–outside relationship. One method is to use an awning extending from the house over a terrace or courtyard (see page 84). Though awnings can be expensive to install, they can double the size of a living room and are an excellent way of accommodating larger gatherings of friends.

Another idea is to have a walkway, which could be open-sided or enclosed with glass, perhaps linking the house to a garage or garden building. If the views to left and right were to be of the garden and perhaps an area of water, a magical inside–out feel could be created, especially when lit at night. The garden on page 127 is an example of this approach.

dissolving walls

Glass walls are now being used to make an instant link between house and garden. They blend well with the contemporary style of interior design, which makes much use of clean, uncluttered materials with simple, well-designed furniture.

Here boundaries are dissolved through the use of large expanses of glass. Although the area is divided into squares, there is a strong sense of continuity running through the design. This is achieved partly by the use of a concrete path and a canal which flow right through the garden. The design reflects the internal proportions of the house, a repetition which is another source of continuity. Planting is restricted to groups of trees of a single variety.

<u>urban sanctuary</u>

<u>above</u>
This garden and conserv-
atory are filled with
brightness and light
despite the small, gloomy
area they occupy. A core
choice of colours and
textures helped to create
the clean, spare look
that I wanted.

How do you bring to life a tiny, dead space alongside a house, especially when it is surrounded by forbidding walls? Turning it into a garden may seem like a fantasy, but the real magic here lies in the addition of a conservatory to make extra living space.

The challenge here was to design a conservatory and garden on top of a small, flat-roofed shop, to divert attention from the rather dreary brick walls and to make the space seem larger. One feature of the view demanded attention: the roof of the adjoining brick church: reminded me of the swooping line of Australia's Sydney Opera House. Consequently I wanted to interfere with this skyward view as little as possible.

The most exciting way to enliven and lighten up the area was to make use of metal for the flooring, garden seating and containers, with corrugated sheeting and mirror glass on the flanking walls. For the walls and floor of the conservatory we used uninterrupted glass – both clear and sandblasted. I couldn't resist keeping one clear panel of glass in the sandblasted floor, and placing beneath it rows of ostrich eggs.

Hardly anyone puts a foot on this clear glass, although in fact it's just as strong as the rest! The clean, graphic feel continues into the garden, where the ground is surfaced in metal grille, and the benches have metal sheeting for their sides and grille for their tops. All the containers are galvanized metal and are simply planted, mainly with evergreens.

The planting between the conservatory and the flanking mirror and corrugated metal walls is carefully contrived to be a continuation of inside, creating ambiguity between indoor and outdoor spaces. The two rows of three tall, galvanized pots placed down each side are infinitely multiplied by their reflections in the mirrored wall. The plants in these pots change seasonally, to give instant colour. In early spring they are filled with white hyacinths, followed by white busy lizzies

below, from left
■ The exterior floor is metal grille, the spaces filled with small pebbles.
■ The view incorporates the nearby church.
■ The ostrich–egg floor panel and single cactus.
■ The light walls and white ceramic vases make wonderful shadows.
■ Box in a container, seen through a side window.
■ Herbs in a trio of metal containers on an indoor window sill.

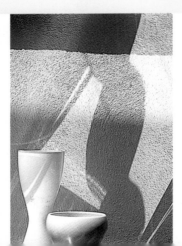

(*Impatiens*). Then perhaps white Longi lilies (*Lilium longiflorum*), followed by white hydrangeas and ornamental cabbages in the autumn – which take us through to the hyacinths early in the year. The feeling of seasonal change in the pots compensates for the evergreen planting outside.

Another contrived inside–outside device is the two clear glass windows in otherwise frosted glass walls. Directly outside are two metal mesh columns, filled with pebbles, on which stand two small galvanized pots, planted with boxwood balls. At night time these pots look rather like three-dimensional pictures in frames.

Inside the conservatory is a single plant – a lovely cactus, very architectural in shape, which is such a statement in itself that nothing more is needed. However, pots of herbs on the kitchen windowsill keep it company.

In the yard the major planting is a series of five small-leafed bamboos, some 6 metres (20 feet) high, all in galvanized containers, the soil topped with pebbles. The reason I wanted them so tall was to break up the surrounding horizontal and vertical lines of the brickwork and fence, and to give a sense of greenery from the internal staircase overlooking the conservatory. The soft green leaves move in the slightest breeze, and from the back bedroom you get the lovely swish of bamboo in the wind, as well as a glimpse of leaves dancing outside the window.

On the left-hand wall is a lovely powder-coated planter-bench, with the two square containers either side planted with grass (they can be used like side tables, to put drinks and plates on). Opposite these is a built-in bench, with a pair of planters containing bamboo on either side, as well as a pair of galvanized pots planted with the wonderful silver-grey, blue hesper palm (*Brahea armata*), with a silver-leaved underplanting of cineraria (*Cineraria maritima*). These look amazing at night, especially as under the metal grille I have placed a blue neon tube, which reflects not only onto the mirror, but also onto the corrugated sheeting on the opposite wall. The down-lighters for the two box balls are attached to a dimmer switch.

below
Planting space is at a premium in this garden, so pots of topiary rosemary and lavender are set on the kitchen doorstep; they also make a useful table centre for outside dining. Their decorative mulch of white gravel is set off brilliantly by the galvanized metal pots.

left
During the summer months potted herbs such as basil, tarragon, thyme, parsley and mint are grown in matching shiny pots on the windowsill. The light casts lovely shadows onto the white-painted walls.

the water feature
consists of water pumped
up a lead pipe into an
old hopper and down a
lead spout into a perspex
basin surrounded by
glass bricks

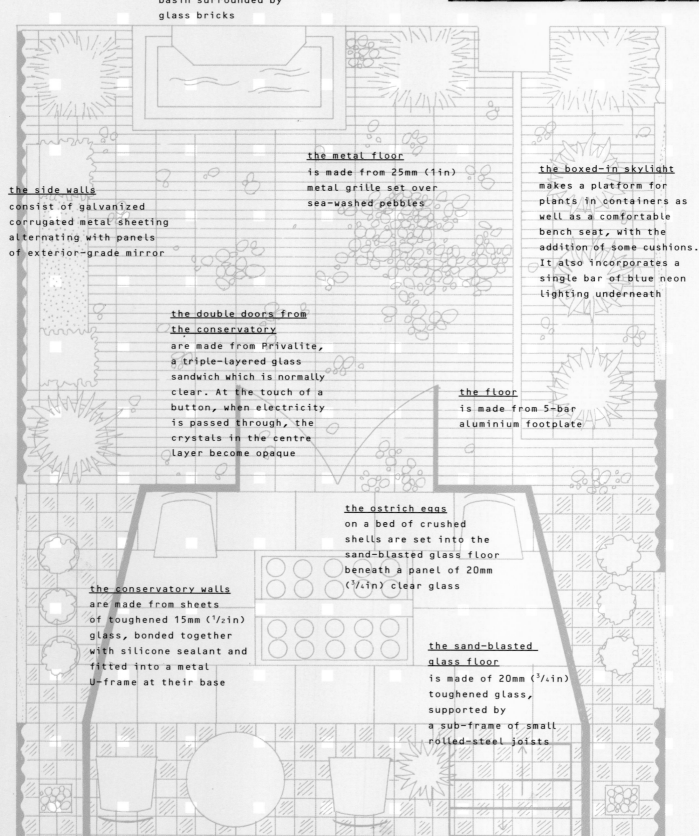

the metal floor
is made from 25mm (1in)
metal grille set over
sea-washed pebbles

the boxed-in skylight
makes a platform for
plants in containers as
well as a comfortable
bench seat, with the
addition of some cushions.
It also incorporates a
single bar of blue neon
lighting underneath

the side walls
consist of galvanized
corrugated metal sheeting
alternating with panels
of exterior-grade mirror

**the double doors from
the conservatory**
are made from Privalite,
a triple-layered glass
sandwich which is normally
clear. At the touch of a
button, when electricity
is passed through, the
crystals in the centre
layer become opaque

the floor
is made from 5-bar
aluminium footplate

134

the ostrich eggs
on a bed of crushed
shells are set into the
sand-blasted glass floor
beneath a panel of 20mm
($^3/_4$in) clear glass

the conservatory walls
are made from sheets
of toughened 15mm ($^1/_2$in)
glass, bonded together
with silicone sealant and
fitted into a metal
U-frame at their base

**the sand-blasted
glass floor**
is made of 20mm ($^3/_4$in)
toughened glass,
supported by
a sub-frame of small
rolled-steel joists

Providing the conservatory with its structural support was the main challenge. We could have removed the roof from the building below and extended the joists to support the new floor, but the cost would have been prohibitive, so instead we laid a frame of rolled-steel joists on top, resting them on the two side walls. This far cheaper option actually broadened the scope of the design. The frame created a void between the new floor and the roof below, so we turned that into a feature.

In the garden area we filled the void with pebbles before laying metal grating on top. This gives a great feeling of space and depth, especially at night when light shines from underneath the conservatory right across the surface of the pebbles. In the conservatory we fitted a sand-blasted glass floor above the void, lighting it from underneath with fluorescent tubes to give an evenly distributed, very white light.

plan & construction

airspace

As new buildings continue to be erected in our cities, outside space becomes ever more valuable. Designers have had to learn to make gardens in minute niches in the urban landscape. A narrow strip of balcony, a well-lit stairwell, or an area of flat roof can all be transformed into tiny urban oases. The screens created by these plantings are an equivalent to the rural hedgerow.

Living on a top floor or in a high-rise flat need not be a bar to having a garden. A balcony or rooftop garden is often a most original space, which comes complete with a dramatic backdrop for the planting. Even the smallest balcony can house a few plants. If you are fortunate enough to look out onto some trees, your plants in the foreground will create a natural link with the planting beyond and give you a much greater feeling of space.

An outdoor space five, ten or more storeys high is in a sense nothing new – even in the Middle Ages there were gardens high on castle battlements and the fabled Ziggurat tower of Babylon is often shown as a series of gardens. The contemporary version is a balcony or roof affording one of the most exciting types of gardening. These gardens present a number of challenges before you can even begin planting. There are constraints such as the availability of space, the load-bearing capacity of the walls and floor and the extremes of temperature caused by too much exposure to sun or wind. Weight will ultimately govern everything else you do, but you must at all costs avoid the common mistake of using tiny containers with very little soil for your plants and then wondering why they don't grow.

above
Hanging pots of colourful flowers suspended from a wooden frame furnish an instant garden in the air.

left
Life among the chimney pots: rooftop gardens offer exhilaratingly varied views and unusual juxtapositions.

realization

One great advantage to having a spacious balcony or roof garden is that it increases the value of your property and this can be a major selling point. But don't go overboard with your budget: I am often asked when designing a roof garden to work out a budget in relation to the value it has added to the property. Before you set your heart on having your garden in the sky, look back to original plans or deeds. Some properties have covenants stating that nothing is allowed in an outdoor space. Even if you have a door onto the space, you may not be allowed to use it. Make sure all these points are addressed before you make detailed plans or spend any money. We have in the past saved clients a lot of heartache by checking out these potential problems at an early stage. However, supposing that you have done all this beforehand, you can begin to plan your outdoor space.

aerial views

Our brief was to design a small outdoor space for this very modern apartment in an elegant, stuccoed building overlooking London's Hyde Park. The aim was to provide a modern design with classical undertones that would tie in with style of the house. We put semi-mature trees in pots on the balcony to provide a link with the park beyond. Looking out across the balcony, one has the sense that the garden goes on for ever and ever.

The elegant planting on this balcony truly complements the gracious surroundings. The effect is wonderfully light and spacious, the feathery leaves of the olive in particular giving lovely dappled shadows on the wall. In such a small space it was important to keep to a limited palette. We used standard eucalyptus, feathered olives, a privet topiary 'cloud' tree and a *Juniperus scopulorum* 'Skyrocket' with clipped box balls and loose, informal planting of *Brachyglottis greyi* and *Helichrysum italicum*.

left
Here the slender forms of junipers echo the distant chimneys, while feathery plants and the wavy line of the planters introduce a soft note against the buildings and terracotta floor tiles laid to represent brickwork.

<u>above</u>
Wire mesh can be cut to patterns as well as being used to support climbing plants. Left whole, this terrace would be too enclosed, giving the feeling of being trapped behind wire. The 'holes' let you get closer to the view over other rooftops.

Plan first for your own individual needs: is your roof garden or balcony to be mainly a green 'oasis', a sun trap, or somewhere to take breakfast or to entertain? If the latter, it is essential to plan space for a table and a pair of, or perhaps four, chairs for dining outside. Their siting will determine the placing and size of any planters; this in turn governs the size of plants that you can grow.

Other practicalities include storage space for hose, implements, fertilizers and perhaps a barbecue and cushions. Irrigation is another factor. I would go so far as to say don't bother to have a roof garden if you haven't got a nearby tap, preferably an outside one, for without a convenient water source gardening on a roof will be no pleasure.

The amount of exposure to wind and strong sunlight will limit the range of plants you will be able to grow. If you can provide shelter by putting up a simple screen sturdy enough to withstand battering by the wind, and if the light levels are reasonably good, you will be able to garden here as anywhere else. The screen could be made from transparent glass or polycarbonate panels. The plants in my own roof garden have to be pretty hardy. I planted tall evergreens that will withstand the exposure, such as oaks (*Quercus ilex*), espaliered pears and olive trees, under-

<u>opposite and above left</u>
In this Japanese-inspired Manhattan rooftop garden designed by Jeff Mendoza to be viewed from inside, the textures vary with each rectangular strip. Between the bronze galvanized steel and the rill of Mexican river stones is a trough of sedums (*S. sexangulare*). The 'pool' is a thin layer of Japanese river stones that catch the sunlight.

above
A tree growing through
the 'roof' of a courtyard
right by the apartments
is a good idea, but always
remember to check the
potential height of the
mature tree. If it begins
to block light from sur-
rounding windows its life
expectancy will be limited.

planted with boxwood. Many city microclimates make it possible to grow plants that are not frost-hardy, for example *Photinia* x *fraseri* 'Red Robin' and *Fatsia japonica*, as well as climbers and grasses. For an oriental-style garden we planted bamboos, which thrive as long as they are kept wellwatered, and assorted pines.

You may want to consider installing an automatic watering system if you have some sizeable containers. I am too busy to spend much time in my own roof garden, but when I can I do enjoy pottering about there, so I turn off the automatic watering system and water by hand. Hand watering also provides an ideal opportunity to examine your plants closely, in order to check for pests. Pest control is very important in an urban environment as cities tend to be a few degrees warmer than the country, which means that fewer bugs are killed off each winter.

I love city skylines but I like them even more when I can distance myself from the view with an expanse of greenery, as with Number 1 Poultry, in London, designed by Arabella Lennox-Boyd (shown below right). I think one of the most effective treatments for a roof is a low, simple panel of grass. Seen sixteen storeys up, it looks really impressive and the surrounding buildings will give you all the drama you need to show off its purity.

I also think a variety of textures can look magnificent, as with Jeff Mendoza's stylish garden above Fifth Avenue, New York, seen on pages 140–1. It is a pool of tranquillity, inspired by pictures of the Ryoan-ji Zen rock garden in Kyoto, Japan. Mendoza had an opportunity to remodel the garden after he'd been to Japan and seen the original. Nestling on a sunny ledge measuring 5.5 x 10 metres (18 x 32 feet), his garden has to cope not only with restrictions of weight, but also with extremes of temperature and buffeting winds. Shrubs had to be situated where their weight could be evenly distributed, such as round the sides, so only plants with a light rootball, such as grasses (*Pennisetum*), could be planted in the gravel area.

The object was to create a satisfying design that holds the onlooker's interest within the garden. This has been achieved by the device of rectangular strips that keep the eye roving in a circular motion. The planting is kept low, with a line of boxwood fringing the parapet and holding off surrounding buildings.

top
A metallic canopy hung from the walkway in a Californian balcony garden throws patches of bright light down onto the table and chairs.

above
In the garden at Number 1 Poultry, by Arabella Lennox-Boyd, parallel lines of box provide a counterpoint to the cityscape verticals.

skyline planting

White flowers up among the rooftops; open skies and clear views above the noise of the street – this is the way to create a real breathing space, a sense of calm and peace in the city. Parapets and planters give shelter to both people and plants.

left
A glimpse of the roof terrace through the cantilevered doorway is enough to lure you outside. A roof space provides an unusual setting for garden plants, such as these white foxgloves.

below, from left
■ The fronts of the pots are uplit at night.
■ Subtle underfloor and uplighting is supplemented by candle light.
■ Ornament of shells and pebbles, collected at the beach, brings memories of a magical day.
■ Containers abut the line of chimney pots.

I am sometimes asked by clients for a garden that is visually exciting, has easy access and ample room for entertaining, and which, once installed, will not cost huge amounts to keep looking seasonally interesting or take too many hours to maintain. These were the criteria I set for my own small roof space, as well as working within a strict budget.

The terrace covers the entire roof space above the property. Originally two roofs sloped to a central gully, so we gained planning permission to change this to a flat roof, and put in the necessary extra strengthening and support. We also added a raised skylight over the bathroom at one side as well as a double central skylight over the master bedroom at the street end. This means that one can lie in bed looking up at the starry sky on a clear night.

Two long side boundaries overlook surrounding roofs, but as yet no-one else nearby has converted their space into a roof garden. At the street end we erected a trellis in Iroko 1 metre (3 feet) inside the front parapet. This was done firstly because I didn't want to draw too much attention to the property for reasons of security, and secondly because it gave the perfect opportunity to grow a plain green ivy screen for total privacy (this end of the terrace is the only one that is overlooked). Access to the remaining roof space at the front is through a matching trellis gate. This part of the roof is a platform giving a bird's-eye view of the street market below, without drawing attention to the building.

The planting has been kept

145

very simple, using mainly ever-greens: eucalyptus, oaks (*Quercus ilex*), olives and box. On the left-hand boundary is a series of four containers, with repeat planting in pairs: espaliered pear trees with cube box trees as underplanting alternate with loose, feathery olive trees with ball box trees to either side. Opposite I placed a single rectangular container with a white-flowering standard wisteria which frames the chimney pots. As a play on the chimney pots, I underplanted it with three boxwood cones.

Lighting is an important factor within this small enclosed garden. I wanted it to appear larger at night-time, but I didn't want to set it ablaze like a lighthouse, so we placed nearly all the light fittings in the floor and uplit the fronts of the containers. At night, the view from the opposite end of the terrace down onto the conservatory garden adds greatly to the drama of the location (see page 135). A final touch, just for fun, was to light the 'borrowed landscape' of a rather lovely church across the rooftops. At one end, where its roof peaks, is a stone owl, put there to ward off pigeons. Using a light beam, I pin-spotted the owl, so that he stands out among the surrounding city slate roofs, looking rather impressive.

147

<u>left</u>
Against the ivy-clad trellis stands a tall cylindrical container planted with a young plume poppy (*Macleaya cordata* 'Kelway's Coral Plume').

<u>right</u>
The round table is placed over a wooden grille housing underfloor lighting. As the bench has its feet and armrests capped in metal, when I bring additional furniture to the roof I use metal chairs from the conservatory. This gives a nice link not only to the bench but also to the Iroko-edged large galvanized planters.

Macleaya cordata
'Kelway's Coral Plume'

the bench
by the larger skylight
stops people getting
too close to it

cylindrical container
with silver-leaved
Senecio cineraria
and seasonal white
foxgloves

the circular timber table
means that one can add
almost any number of chairs
for a lunch or
a dinner party

duckboard square grid
underneath the table has
a fluorescent light box

large square containers
with cone-shaped
evergreen oaks (*Quercus
ilex*) 4-5 metres (12-16
feet) tall, underplanted
with a carpet of box

I first fixed battens over the whole roof area and laid an Iroko deck, giving it a gentle slope into the central drainage gulley, to match the original roof layout and ensure that excess water can be removed quickly. We added a 15cm (6in) skirting board all around the existing 1-metre (3-feet) high boundary wall, a nice detail which finished the edges off neatly and gives the terrace a slightly more interior feel for evening dining. I allowed for the end of the raised bathroom skylight to be timber-clad so that I could turn it into a bench, for a useful additional seating area.

To link in with the wooden floor and to allow air to circulate around the containers (which, being galvanized can become quite hot in direct sunlight), I designed matching Iroko timber frames for all the containers. They form a series of four rectangles along one side, with a pair on the opposite side. A pair of 1-metre (3-feet) square containers stands at the garden end. In between is a tall, circular, heavy-duty galvanized container, which I keep filled with plants for seasonal colour, for instance spring bulbs, white busy lizzies for summer and ornamental cabbages for autumn.

plan & construction

<u>boundaries &</u>   152
<u>screens</u>

<u>surfaces</u>   158

<u>features</u>   162

<u>outside living</u>   169

<u>100 key plants</u>   174

part 3:
directory

Boundaries can be used in the garden in two ways: either to mark the edges of the property
or within the garden itself to divide the space into areas and 'rooms', so creating the
all-important elements of mystery and surprise. Using non-traditional materials such as
mirror glass or galvanized fencing gives an entirely new dimension — best used in combination with brick, concrete and wood, or trained and climbing plants.

boundaries
& screens

below
These granite walls seem
an unlikely setting for
a tree, but form part of
a contemporary garden at
Parc André Citroen, Paris.

WALLS & FENCES

BLOCKWORK see Rendered Walls.

BRICK Old bricks, though they are more expensive than new, in beige or honey-colour through to light and dark terracotta, are always irresistible in the garden where an informal or traditional look is wanted. But to bring the garden more up-to-date, use glazed bricks: though pricier, they come in a huge range of colours, but for choice use subtly coloured ones – I normally prefer to use plain white, though a white or silver-leaved planting against blue or grey glazed bricks is effective. Mortar dye is available so that you can choose a shade to match the bricks, or go lighter or darker. Durable engineering bricks are cheaper and give a harder, more unified feel; they range in colour from rich terracotta red through to a dark grey or black.

Pages 71 112 135 ◀◀

CERAMIC TILES are a cheaper alternative to using glazed bricks to clad a blockwork wall. They usually work most successfully outside if they are all in one colour, with no patterns. But you could introduce evenly spaced narrow tiles in different coloured bands, or alternate same-size tiles in varied colours, with either a horizontal or vertical emphasis. You could also set the tiles inside 'frames' – cladding of a different material. You do need a smooth surface to attach tiles to, i.e. a smooth rendered or plastered wall, using one of the proprietary

glues available for exterior use. Tiling the uprights of steps gives a good effect (page 55), or try lining a dark wall of a courtyard with light-coloured tiles, or the inside of a water feature; you may then need to match the coping in the same style of tiling.

CONCRETE Low concrete walls, especially edgings, up to about 1m (3ft) high and 25cm (10in) thick, need a properly constructed base or footing. This is made by pouring the correct concrete mix of cement and sand into a strong mould (made of timber shuttering). This method means you can make some interesting curvy shapes using plywood (which can bend) for the shuttering, or a zig-zag wall. I would leave such walls plain or paint them with exterior masonry paint, perhaps then painting a design on them using a stencil for a repeat pattern effect (such as

'picket fence', left, which gives an updated *trompe-l'oeil* illusion). You can of course make such a wall more textured (page 50), using coarser sand or fine aggregate.

For higher walls, pre-cast concrete sections set in posts, with side grooves to hold the panels in place, make strong and secure walling. Though these are mostly used on commercial installations, some interesting types can look good in small contemporary town gardens, but they are not the cheapest type of fencing. Usually they are left plain, although they can be painted.

Page 46 ◀◀

CORRUGATED SHEETING is normally supplied in its galvanized form, which is often used as a relatively cheap roofing material on barns and outbuildings. It also comes in a clear plastic form, which we use for fencing or roofing where we want natural light.

It has a smart, clean look, and makes good fencing for internal boundaries or for contrasting with organic forms such as willow-weave. I have also used it for a

roof garden boundary fence (with no objection from the neighbours as it's clean-looking and virtually maintenance free, needing just regular washing with a detergent).

Galvanized sheeting has sharp edges, which we deal with by fixing circular foam insulation (sold for cladding heating pipes) with glue along the top edge as a safety measure. If used vertically as a high boundary, corrugated sheeting needs to be fixed firmly to solid timber posts set in concrete with timber cross-rails. Used horizontally as a low fence, it can be screwed to a small timber frame. Sheet size is approximately 1 x 2m (3 x 6ft).

Page 130 ◀◀

PLASTIC PIPES Lengths of pipe, 1.5-2m (5-6ft) long and 20cm (8in) in diameter, placed together vertically and set into concrete provide a rather unusual solid screen. It's possible to plant them up with small boxwood balls to fit the pipe diameter, or with tall ornamental grasses – they resemble smoke drifting from a chimney. You make the plant container inside by sinking a

153

brick & boulder walls

A brick wall is always satisfying whether left unadorned, used as a foil for plants or as a contrast with other hard materials. Red bricks team particularly well with light-coloured paving, rendered walls and stones. Boulders or pebbles encased in sturdy wire mesh are an idea that has caught on for retaining walls in gardens, using the same technique used for stabilizing motorway embankments – and also buildings (see page 20); I use the same method for making a stand for containers (see page 163). Here the wire mesh is used to support plants, which gives an unusual contrast of colour and texture. One obvious advantage of a wall of small boulders is that they don't need concrete footings or drainage pipes as water can run freely through them.

plastic flowerpot of the right diameter and 45cm (18in) deep to its lip inside the top, and then filling it with compost.

RENDERED WALLS An even, clean rendered surface is most useful for a quick make-over and update for garden walls, and can also cover a multitude of sins – such as old wall repairs, odd brick types or unattractive concrete blockwork. I used this method in the garden on page 86 to give raised beds a streamlined, contemporary look. Leaving the rendering unpainted is popular as it avoids the maintenance problems of a painted wall, and because the natural sand colour is a nice light honey-yellow and gives a pleasing texture. You can of course paint it in plain colours (page 54) or use as a backdrop and paint a design on it.

If the condition of the existing brickwork is not good, it's often cheaper to start with a construction of blockwork rather than render what's already there. You can also smarten up the whole appearance, without going overboard on the budget, by adding a limestone coping (page 93). I like to use willow-weave panels next to natural rendered walls and limestone.
Pages 90 100 ◀◀

STONE CLADDING A wall constructed of blockwork can look great if clad in sections of white limestone or dark granite to give a clean, pure look. The stone is cut into 1cm (1/2in) or thicker panels, depending on size and construction. You could vary this facing by placing one or more mirror panels between the stone sections, glued onto the blockwork, and the cost would be similar. Another good cladding material is panels of York

stone cut to about 1cm (1/2in) thick.
Pages 34 92 121 ◀◀

TIMBER PANEL FENCES come in a range of styles, and the look you choose depends on whether you use hardwood (left natural or varnished) or softwood (painted or stained); both can achieve some pretty stunning effects. One of the best and neatest fences is one of the simplest: a series of upright support posts and two horizontals (arris rails) to which the uprights are nailed; the same method using lower, spaced uprights creates a more open, picket-style fence. This may cost more than fences bought off the shelf, but it gives better quality. Overlap timber panels give most privacy, although they are more expensive.

I often use unprepared softwood panels some 15cm (6in) wide applied to a framework and then stained my favourite pale eucalyptus blue-grey. You can vary the uprights by cutting them to a point, which also makes them more weatherproof, or have a fancy design cut into them; you can also gradually vary the heights of the uprights and shape their tops to form concave (or convex) curves. If you are using prepared (i.e. pressure-treated) softwood, try painting it a bright blue or other colours.

WOODEN GATES, the most usual solid material, can look smart depending on finish and detailing (wood within a metal frame also looks good). They may look best in a natural wood finish to team with natural willow-weave, or colour-stained to team with a similar timber panel fence or trellis. Painting does look really smart but it requires rather more upkeep.

SCREENS & LIGHT FENCING

BALUSTRADES As well as the traditional forms of balustrading (available in reconstituted stone), new versions include those made of toughened glass or stainless steel, though a cheaper type is powder-coated alloy tubular framework (page 92). Steel cable with timber supports every 30cm (12in)

also gives a more contemporary effect, left plain or with plants growing over it.

BAMBOO is a great material for making a light screen, especially made up as squares as an alternative to trellis. Bind each section using natural twine or oiled black

metal screens, fences & canopies

Contrasted with brick and stone, metal is a light, versatile, decorative and also space-saving material for exterior use. *Clockwise, from top left*:
Fence and gate made of steel rods, normally used to reinforce concrete (Chaumont garden festival); galvanized corrugated fencing in a London roof garden; metal panel fencing in a London park playground; traditional black wrought ironwork above the yard gate of a converted school building; a filigree green-painted iron gate makes a good foil for plants; an atmospheric setting for this metal slatted canopy – its vertical poles double as light supports to create strong shadows by night.

powder-coating

This method gives a really contemporary look to metals – especially light alloys – such as balustrading, containers and outdoor furniture. It requires less maintenance and lasts longer than a paint finish, which needs redoing every two to three years, but initially it is about twice as expensive. Of several colours available I prefer a lovely silver-grey with an interesting matt finish, and a deep blue which I used for a fountain. The technique requires a specialist; it can be applied to any rust-free metal surface. Pages 92 170 ◀◀

string, and this will give an oriental feel to it. A more solid bamboo screen can also be made in the same way by setting 10cm- (4in-) diameter bamboo poles of the same length together. Page 48 ◀◀

COPPER PIPING can be used for an unusual internal division, perhaps placed in a diagonal series or in a trellis pattern. It looks great when it oxidizes to verdigris and goes that lovely greenish-blue colour. Page 164 ◀◀

FABRIC Canvas blinds or panels make an effective boundary, particularly on a roof terrace or balcony where occasional extra privacy is needed. They can be attached to railings by eyelets and a rope rigging; white or natural canvas gives an airy feel as it flaps in the breeze, and along roof terrace railings at 1m (3ft) high; it will give you the feeling of being aboard an ocean liner! It is useful as a safety feature, such as wrapped around the outside of a spiral staircase.

For more theatrical effects outdoors, try using mesh or gauzy materials in pure white – or even black – to create small semi-private rooms, such as round a

hot tub, or as a backdrop for planting. Pages 108 113 173 ◀◀

GLASS PANELS & PANES are another screening that people are learning to use, now that glass is not a building material to be scared of, as long as it is fitted by a specialist. I use sandblasted glass panels as a boundary between extruded alloy posts. At night this looks truly amazing, lit from behind. A variation (though expensive) is to use a wall of sandblasted panels with one or two clear windows in them, so that you can look directly into another part of the garden with plants on the other side (page 131), and is great lit up at night.

If you wanted to give a certain area in your garden, or your roof terrace, some protection, without obscuring the surroundings, I would recommend using 'Victorian' wire glass, a great security window or door glass, which has a squared mesh of wire sandwiched between two glass panels. 'Privalite' glass is made up of three layers, the central panel being covered in crystals that react when electricity is passed through them, to turn otherwise clear glass opaque. This gives you the flexibility of creating privacy at certain times.

It is an expensive treatment, but also very smart and practical. Pages 52 156 ◀◀

GLASS BLOCKS & BRICKS are ideal for creating internal boundaries, as they come not only in clear glass but also frosted or coloured, which can produce some stunning, very graphic effects. They look superb as a panel within a length of rendered wall, especially with rear light shining through them.

For constructions using glass blocks I would always consult a structural engineer for advice on the most appropriate method for fixing as safety is of utmost importance, and they are not cheap to buy. Pages 156 167

HURDLES are simply low woven fencing made from natural willow or hazel, using much thicker stems than willow-weave, although the stems split to make them more flexible to use. The sections of fencing, usually of a standard size (1 x 2m or 2 x 2m/3 x 6ft or 6 x

6ft), last five to six years. They are fixed by positioning self-support poles with pointed ends in the ground, or, for taller hurdles, by attaching the panels to support posts. They are useful for giving protection to a planting of shrubs or young trees until they mature, and can be removed once they deteriorate. Pages 66 68 92 ◀◀

METAL GATES are designed in some of the best contemporary styles I've seen, sometimes as pieces of sculpture in their own right, sometimes to reflect a particular theme or planting used in the garden. Different finishes may be applied to an iron base which may be galvanized, painted or powder-coated (page 155). Tubular steel and angle iron are also effective as they can easily be made to specific requirements in a variety of styles. Page 154 ◀◀

METAL PANEL FENCING comes with a variety of meshes and panels, and even tubular pipes.

wiring for security

Chain-link wire fencing such as that used for tennis courts is nowadays usually available as plastic-coated wire mesh and is supported between iron posts sunk into a concrete base. At 2-2.5m (8-10ft) high it is a most perfect security fence, but requires plants to be grown over it to improve its appearance and to provide any privacy. It is available uncoated in a galvanized finish, but normally comes in either green or black which, set behind a well-planned shrub or flower border, all but disappears.

Metal 'curly-wurly' is a great-looking, relatively inexpensive security wire for placing along the tops of walls to stop people climbing over. The bonus is that it's as good-looking as a piece of sculpture. One could grow plants over it, but great care would be needed when doing routine maintenance, as the 'curls' are very sharp.

translucent screens

Both solid glass and the flimsiest materials have a place in contemporary garden design, anywhere you need to place a windbreak and also avoid cutting out too much light.

Clockwise, from top left:

Stiffened plastic mesh giving a sculptural touch with stems; 'fairground fish' hung up with plastic sheeting from a rail (both Chaumont garden festival); coloured portholes (by Martha Schwartz, see page 46); translucent glass block screen in a rendered wall; sandblasted glass screen (by Robert Grace); and a 'water screen' (at Chaumont).

156

It provides the security of a solid fence without total loss of view and light, as well as having great versatility in design. It can be supplied as galvanized, rectangular mesh which you then need to support between upright timber or steel posts. It is far from cheap but so indestructible that it is worthwhile in the long run.
Page 154 ◀◀

METAL RAILINGS, traditionally made from iron and painted black, are now more often made of galvanized metal and steel in a host of colours and designs, such as the updated wavy fence on

page 47; aluminium fencing is also on the market. You can paint or powder-coat plain metal to suit. Iron railings, still the most expensive, were the favoured way of dealing with a front boundary (until the two world wars demanded their use for munitions), placed along a low wall or a ground-level stone lintel. Black remains the most used colour (it was Prince Albert who declared that all railings and gates should be painted black), but the tops tend to align with the top horizontal rather than the old spear-shape.

PERSPEX & POLYCARBONATE are appearing more and more in gardens: as fencing they are useful as plants can grow close up to them, for they allow light from both sides. I have used white and frosted Perspex for boundaries to allow maximum light into an area, yet still provide privacy. It is now available in bright colours and also black – which I cannot wait to have the opportunity of using – but these can work out rather expensive. We also use semi-opaque corrugated plastic for translucent but sturdy fencing.

PICKET FENCING is formed from posts and arris rails with alternating uprights and spacers, and is much-used for cottage-style and New England colonial-style gardens. It also has a strong place in the contemporary garden, but is used there more as an internal division fence, especially when painted in bright colours.
Page 91 ◀◀

PLASTIC makes an interesting screen, either as light, transparent mesh or a heavier, opaque material, usually stretched and sewn over an alloy support; it is inexpensive, readily available and easy to replace (see left).

TRELLIS in hardwood or softwood is available as small 10cm (4in) squares, large 15cm (6in) squares, or in rectangles or diamond patterns (my least favourite), in a variety of frame shapes and sizes. However, the price of the more decorative, curved designs may be a deciding factor. Plain rectangular or square panels are not at all difficult to make yourself. For a quick makeover, I tend to use trellis made of softwood, either stained or painted. (I think it is a shame to stain or paint hardwood, as its

natural beauty is enough; I always seal or varnish it.) Trellis can be used for high screens but this doesn't suit all gardens, and I find people now want more solid boundaries for security as well as privacy. I do like to use trellis along the top of a solid wall, both to soften its appearance and to give an extra bit of height to grow plants on. It's also excellent for internal garden divisions and for plant supports along a house wall.

Some interesting effects come from mixing different sizes of square trellis, for example in alternating panels, or placing a 'window' within it; against a wall this can give an interesting *trompe-l'oeil* effect of space continuing.
Page 78 ◀◀

WILLOW-WEAVE PANELS are one of my most favourite materials to work with in a garden; they can be made to any shape or size or bought as ready-made standard-size panels. They are woven from slender willow stems, up to 1.5cm (1½in) diameter and about 1.5m (5ft) long, in a simple basket-weave pattern. For a typical rustic look, I nail them to support poles of willow or for a flatter, squarer, more contemporary image, on a square timber frame. I love putting willow-weave next to metal such as 10cm- (4in-) square galvanized posts or a nickel-plated framework (see also Containers, page 166). I also use willow-weave for fill-in panels between the timber supports of a summerhouse, or even to disguise an ugly roof. As a fencing material its price is about the same as overlap panel fencing, but its lifespan is no more than six to eight years. It is a useful temporary screen for privacy while a hedge is growing, or to give protection to a border.
Pages 68 – 92 ◀◀

PLANTED SCREENS

ESPALIERS & PLEACHED TREES These methods give a raised hedge effect with a more open look. You need to build a framework by training young trees (traditionally fruit trees) using wire and pole supports (see below). Ready-shaped 2- to 3-year-old trees are available from nurseries, but careful pruning will be required throughout the tree's life. Pleaching requires patience for it will take a decade or so to achieve a 2m (6ft) clear stem, with a further 2m (6ft) of joined branches to form the raised hedge; again, this is achieved by tying the branches to thin horizontal poles. Pleached limes are a way of forming a high-level boundary, so long as you appreciate their bare-leaved, skeletal appearance in winter.

Pages `78` `86` ◀◀

HEDGING, even planted with evergreens, is often cheaper than a man-made boundary. There are two options for buying hedging plants, depending partly on the number of plants needed for the length of hedge you require. If you can afford large containerized stock you will achieve an instant look, but any plant, even box, is expensive to put in already established at much higher than 30cm (12in). Also, large, older plants are less likely to thrive than young, bare-rooted saplings planted in autumn or early spring, so bare-rooted stock is a better and cheaper option, though the final result will take longer. Smaller plants will often establish sooner and grow on more quickly.

Beech (*Fagus sylvatica*) and Hornbeam (*Carpinus betulus*) are popular deciduous hedging plants, as they can be shaped so easily. After five or so years they will easily reach 3–5m (10–15ft). They keep their rust-brown leaves through the winter months, and need clipping only once a year.

Box (*Buxus sempervirens*) is usually grown for low hedging but I have seen it at almost 2m (6ft) high. It needs clipping at least twice a year, often more.

Holly (*Ilex* sp.) acts as good security hedging and, once fully established at 2m (6ft), is a barrier to be reckoned with, although it's not the cheapest, nor the fastest-growing hedge plant.

Laurel (*Prunus lusitanica*) provides a lovely thick, quite fast-growing hedge which shapes well, but looks best if carefully hand-pruned; it is relatively inexpensive.

Privet (*Ligustrum* sp.) is an evergreen plant I would like to see used more in gardens, for it has a softer and looser habit than box.

Viburnum (laurustinus, V. *tinus*) is worth using as it responds well to clipping.

Yew (*Taxus baccata*) is the classic among evergreens with its lovely dark green leaves; it needs clipping once a year, in summer.

Pages `41` `178-9` ◀◀

TOPIARY SCREENS Shrubs and trees planted in a row and clipped to regular matching shapes is an alternative to solid hedging.

Plants with a naturally formal habit, such as *Juniperus scopulorum* 'Skyrocket', or trained mop-heads such as privet look great, though yew and box are the classics.

Pages `40` `179` ◀◀

157

trained plants

Plants trained along wires or poles, or as self-supporting shapes, either as espaliers or woven willow screens (see page 44) are good where space is limited as they are narrower than hedging. Fast-growing ivies are ideal as they keep their foliage, as are evergreen honeysuckles and clematis. Wires or a wire mesh grid, free-standing or against a wall, are the most cost-effective method where plants need support. Softwood trellis is the usual alternative, fixed by nailing trellis frame to battens screwed to the wall or a self-supporting frame. Bamboo and willow can also be made up like a trellis frame; their natural colour looks good in a square symmetrical design on a black-painted wall, as it gives something traditional with a contemporary 'look'. Wires are good for a painted wall, because when you repaint, the wires are cut and the plants laid down; after repainting, fix new wires and reattach the plants. Use galvanized hooks and wires spaced horizontally, every 30cm (12in).

From left to right:

A living willow framework is trained to an oval with a hoop support; a young pleached lime tree, showing the structure of wires and canes; a topiaried espalier fruit tree; a tunnel of morning glory on a curved metal pergola; and wire-trained ivy making a filigree roof screen.

Hard surface areas in particular need to be sympathetic to the house or other adjacent buildings in terms of style and materials. Tiles, marble and slate, formerly considered more suited to inside use, as well as glass and metal plate, are now being recognized as excellent outdoor surfaces, while lawns are becoming more geometric, often combined in rectangles or curves to contrast with paved materials.

<u>surfaces</u>

<u>below</u>
Regular tiles of slate, interplanted with moss, create a 'landscape' patchwork rather like fields and hedgerows from the air.

PAVINGS, CONCRETE & GRAVEL

BRICKS are a great, traditional, hard-wearing material for paths and surface areas but they will not give you that up-to-date look; give them a contemporary edge by laying a surround of limestone. Or use the bricks as edgings, to set off stone materials or planting.

House bricks, however, are not suitable for paving as they soak up water and deteriorate with frost; for garden surfaces you must use well-fired bricks, facing bricks or industrial bricks. I always try to use bricks that colour-match either the house or other features in the garden.

Pages **68** **112** ◀◀

COBBLES, in light greys and white, look good as a decorative surface either in informal drifts with loose planting, or as regular edgings or squares, laid on edge around containers. They are not good for walking on unless they are set half in concrete. As an inexpensive material they are useful and look fresh for a quick makeover.

Pages **44** **47** ◀◀

CONCRETE SLABS are available in a multitude of sizes and colours, some textured or even with a gravel layer, others completely plain. It is the lighter colours that work most stylishly with planting schemes generally, although I have used black ones (rather like slate) successfully. Buy good quality square or rectangular slabs (quality does vary and cheap ones really do look nasty). Do avoid using concrete slabs that look like bricks on edge or patterned slabs – neither works well.

Page **65** ◀◀

GLASS CHIPPINGS are available as small, rounded pebbles for paths, and come in clear, frosted or coloured forms, which all reflect the light in a quite unique way. Treat them in the same way as gravel – they need a firm base of hardcore and sand.

Pages **160** ◀◀

GRANITE SLABS or setts are best used with a slightly rough-cut finish to the surface for safety underfoot. I use granite for covering small areas in urban gardens or as edging between planting and lawn or driveways. I prefer a lovely dark grey granite that works well with a silver and white planting scheme, and equally well with a red-themed planting.

GRAVEL see Stone Chippings.

METAL A metal grille such as lionweld kennedy (galvanized steel) makes a wonderfully graphic surface, with the spaces in between filled with gravel. It does require the ground to be level, and will be a 'flat shoes only' area! The grille also makes for interesting walkways and, as it is galvanized, requires no maintenance. Finer grades are also available. Metal sheeting can look really glamorous, especially for an area connecting an interior and exterior space, but needs a non-slip finish.

Pages **130** **140** ◀◀

PAVERS come in a variety of shapes and so are best for achieving irregular shapes and curves. I love doing whole driveways with pavers, as they are warmer in effect than tarmac and only a little more expensive. Apart from the basic squared shape, they come in different wedge shapes to fit curved edges, which give a lovely organic flow to a hard surface, especially around a mature tree or feature plant.

See below.

POURED CONCRETE can be made to look interesting by the way in which it is laid or finished off. The expansion joints (a necessary part of all surfaces or walls made with concrete) can be a feature in themselves, incorporating geometric lines or curves. Also, when the concrete is setting (the term is 'going off'), you can brush the top to expose the aggregates (coloured gravel, used in the sand mix) for a much richer effect. Another interesting surface is achieved by setting thick bamboo canes into the wet cement mix at 10cm (6in) intervals as it is going off – it makes a most attractive path.

Pages **129** **160** ◀◀

RECONSTITUTED STONE looks great used in squares and has a clean, precise feel. It can be manufactured to specific sizes, to be laid to a specific design. It is easier to lay, and much cheaper, than specially cut natural stone, which has become much less available and more costly.

Page **64** ◀◀

SLATE is a lovely material to use and gives a smart, contemporary appearance laid in rectangles or squares. Slate becomes slippery

159

bricks & pavers

Bricks, and also slabs and pavers, can be set into sand or, for a firmer base, a sand and cement mix. They always look better with a contrasting edging.

From left to right: A well-laid brick path is always irresistible, especially edged in stone; a double row of brick makes a clean edge to the paving; bricks inset in concrete allow for a varied layout; square pavers are ideal for curved areas.

pebbles & chippings

There's far more to gravel than buff or grey-coloured stones! Colour apart, there are new materials ranging from slate to recycled plastic and even glass. Clockwise, from top left:
Blue plastic chippings made from recycled materials; Traditional gravel contrasted with an area of green glass 'grass'; a few pebbles make an effective surround and 'dressing' for a bubble fountain; grey slate slabs and chippings are a great foil to this *Senecio cineraria* (syn. *Cineraria maritima*).

when wet, so it is not advisable to use it for a whole path, especially with youngsters or the elderly about. But it sets off metal galvanized containers particularly well, and is good for blending with other materials – try setting slate slabs between gravel or even slate chippings.
Page 158 ◄◄

STONE CHIPPINGS and gravel

have plenty of scope in a contemporary context. Cotswold stone chippings with their warm honey-buff tones are so sympathetic to planting, but for stunning effects I use different coloured gravels from dazzling white to stark black. Slate chippings give a soft grey look that is stunning with a red or silver planting scheme.

STONE PAVING York stone was

once the preferred hard surface for great gardens the world over, but is now extremely costly; much of that still available is recycled, for example from street pavements. For an updated look, I love to use it machine-cut into clean rectangular or square sections, sometimes as a border to 'finish' a terrace of uneven, irregular York stone, or with the whole terrace laid to limestone and edged with

squared York stone. All stone needs regular cleaning to prevent it becoming slippery when wet.

TIMBER used for surfaces in gardens is more or less limited by availability and cost, and this is very much linked to environmental considerations. One must be aware now of the extent of illegal plundering of forests, especially the tropical teak forests, which are being rapidly swept away for use in the gardens of the West. Teak is so scarce that price alone now virtually prohibits its use, and it's not always possible to be certain of the provenance of wood sold with an 'eco-friendly' label. We did use it on a couple of installations and it does look truly amazing, with a really smart finish.
Pages 105 118 149 ◄◄

160

timber used for decking & paths

We mainly use Iroko, pine and Western Red cedar as these woods are grown commercially. Recycled timbers, such as old railway sleepers are an alternative, although these are becoming expensive because of their popularity. But they do look good in garden areas around converted warehouses or factory buildings, and as retaining walls for beds; they also make good, heavy-duty plant containers.

Iroko has a natural oil within the timber, and keeps its rich honey colour if you continue oiling it. It turns silver-grey quickly if you leave it to weather. It's a much cheaper alternative to teak and we use it mainly for decking roof gardens.
Pine is an interesting wood to use for decking, but creates more of a rustic finish, especially if the wavy-edge bark of the tree is left on the wood when it is sawn into planks; this does leave small spaces in the planking, which I turn to advantage by planting ferns or moss in the gaps.

Western red cedar is at a mid-range price. It looks most effective when colour-stained, but if left weathers well to a silver-grey colour, similar to Iroko.

From left to right: Light pine decking on a roof terrace reflected in mirror glass; decking abuts a sand and cement path; decking steps through a marshland garden; bamboo poles set in a concrete screed are excellent for grip on sloping paths; this path makes use of thin slats set in opposing directions; Iroko bridge over a 'dry' pebble stream.

INTERIOR
– EXTERIOR

ORGANIC
MATERIALS
& LAWNS

ALUMINIUM is just starting to become more widely recognized as a great material for outdoor flooring. I use 3- and 5-bar aluminium footplate as an inside–outside material in a conservatory and for steps (see above).
Page 133 ◀◀

GLASS is a material people are gradually becoming less afraid of using outside; I have made a whole glass floor for an inside–outside conservatory. For safety, use only less slippery, ribbed glass; it is slightly more expensive than York stone. I like placing glass bricks with lighting beneath them in between ordinary floor bricks – it looks very effective. All sorts of ideas stem from the ostrich eggs under glass.

The same clear glass can be used outside, for example using a drain inspection frame designed for paving but using glass panels. It could be filled with interesting objects of your own choosing.
Page 130 ◀◀

MARBLE SLABS, especially the lightest cream or white marble, are good for introducing a Mogul theme to your garden yet still give a modern look. If you are using black marble, a polished square with a white pebble surround would look stunning, and is cheaper than using only marble. A rough natural cut is advisable, or use it polished with cut tread lines to reduce slip. The great thing about marble is that it requires hardly any maintenance.
Pages 93 163 ◀◀

RUBBER MATTING for outdoor use is available in various raised designs, such as dots, which act as a safety feature if it is wet, and in bright colours and black, which I have used in conjunction with a limestone pathway. It is available on a roll and can easily be cut to size, and is held in place with a strong adhesive. Alternatively, it is available as sheeting, in many colours from bright primaries to muted shades. This is mainly used for children's play areas, as it absorbs the shock of a fall. It can work well for pathways and patios, and is nice to walk on in bare feet. Laying it is a specialist procedure as it comes in large rolls. It is also available in a grainy surface rather like tarmac, in various colours.

TILES make excellent indoor–outdoor flooring, but those used for the garden must be of exterior quality, which makes them expensive. If they are shiny they may be slippery and look out of place. Malt-glazed tiles, with rough or textured finishes, are one solution and have a lovely natural colour. Small patterned tiles laid in a continuous design can be run from inside to outside and even cope with curves (see page 138). Terrazzo tiles (made from ground marble and stone) can look unbelievable and are just possibly worth their very high cost because of the wonderful colours available. Tiles are heavy and must be laid into a sand and cement screed on a concrete base.
Pages 54 65 138 ◀◀

AROMATIC LAWNS made from thyme (_Thymus_ sp.) or camomile (_Chamaemelum nobile,_ syn. _Anthemis nobile_) planted in a compact area and walked on occasionally will, when trodden on, give off the most amazing scent. Small-leaved, low-growing, creeping and mat-forming varieties are best for this purpose, such as silver-leaved thyme _T. x citriodorus_ 'Silver Queen' which has a stunning lemony scent or camomile _C.n._ 'Treneague' which is non-flowering and less shaggy. Or mix varieties of thyme for a 'tapestry'.

BARK CHIPPINGS are a good, cost-effective way of defining pathways, or even children's play areas, and are readily available at garden centres. They must be laid on a good sub-base of hoggin (crushed stone) or they will easily turn into a mud slurry. Areas also need to be edged to stop the chippings migrating into flower beds or onto other hard surfaces.

GRASS LAWNS are the most commonly used ground covering in any garden, as grass is so versatile. It is also great for setting for sculpture, though designers are even using grass shapes and mounds to form sculpture (see above and page 15). I tend to design lawns with straight edges, but geometric curves also give a contemporary image. Grass mixes so well with other surfaces – such as timber or lengths of limestone for a walkway. Different types of grass seed are available depending on the lawn's purpose and

where you want to sow it. Some mixes are for shady areas, others for tough lawns (for play or sports), and for the best soft carpet, a lawn like a bowling green. Sowing seed on meticulously prepared soil is the best way to achieve a good long-term lawn, although laying turf does give an instant effect.
Pages 15 42 94 96 ◀◀

lawn geometry

Lawns need never be boring, as these images show:
above: turf arrow by Dale Joseph Rowe; _below_: grass and granite steps at Park André Citroen; _bottom_: curves against limestone.

Decorative features or small design details are often the most memorable things about a garden and are entirely subjective. But there are clues to good positioning, especially in a small garden that may lack vistas: a strong statement — at a focal point — perhaps a sculpture, a bowl or even large pebbles. Water adds something else — movement and sound.

features

FOCAL POINTS

ARCHES & PERGOLAS are always eye-catching features, but in turn they draw attention to the vista they frame. They are useful devices for linking one part of the garden to another, or alternatively for creating the feeling of separate spaces, even in small gardens.

A simple arch gives a feeling of scale and is a useful 'anchor' for a planting scheme (page 64). For a more contemporary look use metal, copper piping, guttering, bamboo, steel iron, aluminium, plastic-coated metal or even fishing net (page 39). Posts need to be well-founded in a concrete base; for square timber posts metal supports hammered into the ground are available. If you grow plants over them, most effective is to use repeat planting (page 32). I much admired a pergola I saw at the Getty Museum in Los Angeles made of simple lilac-painted timber and planted with an almost matching mauve-flowering *Wisteria sinensis*. Pergolas are also a good way to create shade.

Pages 54 64 157 ◀◀

COLUMNS (page 42 and far right) are useful for creating a strong vertical, perhaps in place of a tree, or to hold up a roof structure. Old stone or wood columns can often be bought as salvage items and brought up to date used in conjunction with metal or glass. Also, lengths of clear, white or coloured perspex and even strengthened glass, square in cross section, look great uplit from underneath. I also make pebble columns, with the pebbles contained inside wire mesh to make a circular or rectangular block 1m (3ft) or more high, to double up as a plant pedestal.

GAZEBOS A free-standing open structure, something between a pergola and a garden pavilion, gives the feel of an enclosed space (often with a solid roof for shelter). Its original purpose was to offer a resting place with a view after a long walk from the main house. Wrought iron and other metals are available in contemporary designs, as are trellis gazebos designed to match pergolas. Why not use more adventurous materials, such as sections of willow-weave or bamboo poles?

Page 154 ◀◀

MIRRORS can achieve some amazing effects, especially in small gardens where space is limited. By placing a mirror to reflect opposite boundaries, you can lengthen perspective (page 33); it works even better at one end of a rill of water. Mirror glass, as a hard material, also looks great in sections between corrugated sheeting (page 130). Because mirrors are always a focal point they must be used carefully, especially if placed in an arch or at the end of a path – you should always use a thick grade of mirror glass for safety reasons.

OBELISKS similar to columns but often tapered and suitable for growing plants over, these provide a welcome vertical accent used either singly or in pairs. Ready-made in metalwork or self-built in wood or bamboo, they can form a decorative feature in their own right, without being covered by plant material. To add height, structure and a three-dimensional feel to a small space, simply made trellis 'pylons' are easily constructed (page 53). They look great uplit at night. For trellis features, I tend to use timber square trellis made from Iroko or Western red cedar; softwoods such as pine I usually colour stain to link it to the theme of the garden: perhaps a washed-out grey-green eucalyptus colour or a light silvery-blue; either would work well with a silver-grey, green and white planting colour scheme.

Page 164 ◀◀

SALVAGE ITEMS These are any old or odd items, maybe plaques or objects that I can mount into a rendered or painted masonry wall, or place in a small garden area or courtyard which needs a central feature. Ordinary household items can be transformed into features, such as the towering 'bottle spouts' on page 164.

Quite often at weekends I find myself going around reclamation yards looking for special objects, such as an old lead wall hopper from Manchester Fire Station. This I mounted on a back wall, attaching a lead pipe to turn it into a fountain with a glass brick pool beneath to hold the water.

Page 167 ◀◀

163

non-traditional structures

Any noteworthy structure can become an exciting addition to the garden, or perhaps the one element that centres the whole garden design. It doesn't have to be costly, just imaginative.

Clockwise, from top left:
A metal and mesh frame painted with hammerite, with a glass ball finial, makes a decorative strawberry cage and central feature in a kitchen garden; stone columns perch like a classical temple by a lake shore, the sky reflected in a black marble floor; shadow play with a row of hazel plant obelisks, too striking as sculptures to be covered in plants; an octagonal 'room' formed by black pipes supporting black net transforms a planting of dahlias into an exotic experience.

small eye-catchers

In any garden it's good to create little surprise happenings tucked into odd corners, or at the junction of paths, or perhaps half-hidden in a circle of longer grass in the middle of a lawn. *Clockwise, from top left*: A willow-weave wigwam covered with nasturtiums and sweet peas growing in a galvanized container; heads, complemented by the great leaves of *Petasites japonica*, form part of a sculpture 'Members of the Committee' at the Hannah Peschar sculpture garden; a contemporary copper sundial; copper piping looking wonderful with tall, coppery grasses in an installation by Bonita Bulaitis; junk in the form of plastic water bottles cleverly transformed into a series of water spouts.

SCULPTURE is not used in gardens as much as it could be; it can include any object, or simply a grouping of stones or pieces of wood that give personal satisfaction or have some personal significance. I love putting a really modern piece of sculpture in an old-established garden, or conversely a classical-style figure, a sundial or astrolabe in a cleanly minimalist, modern garden. Either of these give a sense of surprise, which is what placing sculpture should be about. I like placing a form right in the middle of a planted border, something to spark the imagination, like the copper pipes (see above), but I also like to place objects as focal points in obvious places, like the end of a pathway or at a junction of two pathways. Good lighting of such features with spotlights or uplighters (page 172) is important. Sculpture can also play a major part in the creation of the whole concept of the garden, as at the Chaumont garden festival where 'Richochets', a series of steel rods with pebbles bolted on top are positioned in drifts (page 37); or the rough-cut, vertical limestone panels create the atmosphere of a mountainside in mist (page 162).

STEPS are so often thought of simply as a necessity in the garden, but they create such a strong design statement that they should be used to best advantage in terms of placing and materials. Even the simplest concrete or stone steps can be transformed by a row of three containers with repeat planting.

SUMMERHOUSES & GARDEN PAVILIONS, and also sheds for garden storage, can be turned into decorative features. They must be well positioned and given an identity to link with your overall design: to keep the symmetry of one such scheme, I insisted on a pair of sheds rather than one (both are used fully, despite the client's initial scepticism). If made in wood I like to see these features painted in bright, bold colours. An all-glass pavilion can look wonderful, as with the riverside pavilion on page 22 and in the park on page 28.

SUNDIALS are traditional in gardens and, as well as the circular stone ones with a metal dial raised on a stone plinth, some beautiful sculptural types are now available made of metals such as copper, brass, glass and mirror glass.

See also: **Containers** page **165**; **Water** page **166**; and **100 Key Plants** page **174** ◀◀

steps

These all hold their own in style and atmosphere. Left to right: cool stone up to a gazebo at Parc André Citroen; red concrete contrasting with planting; steps in gravel at right angles to a water rill by Ron Lutsko; broad steps along a terrace.

PLANTERS & CONTAINERS

CONCRETE PIPES can provide some unusual planters. I use short lengths of pipe planted up, sinking a whole row of five or more of them into the ground. They make a good foil to grasses such as *Festuca glauca*, or the black 'grass' *Ophiopogon* (page 182). More dramatic effects using concrete are achieved by constructing built-in containers with wavy walls; this can be done by pouring concrete into formwork (shuttering) made from sheets of ply bent into the desired shape. I also build terraces of square concrete boxes in a series of seven, varying their heights and diameters.

COPPER & POLISHED ALUMINIUM are two really lovely materials to work with. I have used copper mostly to add detail to other containers, but have wrapped some square containers in copper sheet, which looks really effective. Polished aluminium, a relatively new material, creates a really wonderful effect.
Pages 59 132 ◀◀

GALVANIZED containers have the best contemporary look – and are almost my trademark. They are made from sheets of galvanized iron, formed into cylinders, squares or rectangles, up to 60cm (24in) diameter or width. Anything larger (and they can be up to diameter or width 150cm/5ft and more), should be made of mild steel dipped in galvanized coating. Rectangles and long troughs need internal supports added, otherwise they lose their shape. I like using heavy-duty rectangular containers with an Iroko-wood frame detailing.
Pages 53 101 131 133 144 ◀◀

GLASS BLOCKS OR BRICKS have long been a favourite material for containers, and also for an opaque glass water feature fed by a water spout (page 167). We made matching square plant containers using clear glass bricks of the same size, and it has become a talking point to see the root systems growing. Both pool and plant containers are designed with perspex liners to prevent freezing water or soil moisture expanding the joints in winter which might crack the glass.

LEAD containers have been used for many years for plants, and fortunately there are still many good craftsmen working in lead. Again, I prefer plain designs and rectangular or square shapes that keep the line simple and clean. Be warned – lead is extremely heavy and is unsuitable for balconies and roof terraces.

PLASTIC is widely used for ornamental pots and their quality has improved vastly – it's possible to buy plastic 'terracotta' that you actually have to knock to see if it is real clay or not. Plastic is perfect for balconies or roof terraces, when weight loading has to be taken into consideration.

container tips

Use pots as big as the space can take. Plants then have plenty of room for new root growth, and enough depth of soil to prevent them drying out too quickly.
Try to use up-to-date finishes that avoid the maintenance of, say, ordinary paint, such as galvanizing and powder-coating. If you don't underplant your shrubs, use a decorative mulch for a uniform finish such as small pebbles or gravel of one colour, or bark, to deter weeds and retain moisture (pages 92, 133).

165

RAISED BEDS Sometimes, when we are designing a small garden, or where the depth and quality of the soil is not very good, we put in raised beds to add depth to the soil. These can be made of timber or concrete, perhaps stone-clad, rendered or painted (see Concrete, page 153). If they are high enough, the edges can be used for seating. Including built-in planters will also give the garden body and structure and even provide its main hard landscaping.
Pages 86 128 ◀◀

STONE CONTAINERS Various companies (see Suppliers) produce good reconstituted stone containers in various different shades, which are of course, though still costly, cheaper than antique ones. I tend to use a mellow cream turning to a grey (the colour of Bath stone). I prefer to use plain pots wherever possible and avoid those with fancy reliefs, swags

planted water features

From left to right: I loved this idea of using floating woven baskets, lined with polythene and filled with soil, to grow lettuces in (it should keep them away from slugs); a star-shaped concrete container 'floating' in a lily pond; a similar idea on a grander scale with clipped *Magnolia grandiflora*; an old drinking trough given new life.

and animals etc. You can create a pebble-lined container using the filled mesh technique (page 20); the container is created by placing the mesh round a smaller rectangular perspex box, and infilling the space with pebbles.

Pages 92 100 ◀◀

TERRACOTTA POTS have increasingly adventurous designs and I admit to a liking for ribbed rectangular ones for window boxes as well as large, plain, square containers. Regular, round terracotta pots look good with basket-weave patterning around the outside. The only problem with terracotta is that salt deposits sometimes appear through the pot; an alternative is to use terracotta 'look-alike' plastic.

Pages 30 60 ◀◀

WILLOW-WEAVE CONTAINERS We developed a willow sleeve, mainly to soften the appearance of galvanized pots. These either cover the metal completely, or wrap around the top and bottom

of the container. The willow wraps can be made to any size; I used them for 1.2m (4ft) high and 1m (3ft) diameter containers planted with 2.5m (8ft) high bay trees.

WOODEN containers or planters have been used for centuries, and the best known is the classic Versailles box, a square container with an upright in each corner, topped with a ball detail. Usually painted white, but can be left natural or colour-stained, and easy to make to match or link with decking, or alternatively use plain wooden boxes of rough-sawn timber.

Marine ply is an interesting man-made timber for short-term installations; it looks more decorative if you stain it with a coloured wood stain linked to your design. We tend to use it most often to make window boxes or similar containers. The fibrous look of the timber is made more interesting by staining or varnishing, but it's not the most sophisticated look.

Page 41 ◀◀

container impact

It can't be said often enough that pattern and repetition are the way to ensure a cohesive design, and three or more smaller pots have more impact than one large one. Keep planting simple and, as here, go for repeat planting rather than variety.
From left to right: The trees are planted in the ground and the baskets lend more impact; containers also look good when raised up, as along this wall, or on a plinth or low table; these grasses (*Carex*) look dazzling against their polished aluminium containers.

WATER

FOUNTAINS where the water appears to come straight from the ground can be just as effective as those set in a large expanse of water. At Park André Citroen, lines of fountains set on a slope rise and fall, row by row, in a fantastic display, via a computer-generated programme; the water simply flows down to a grille.

At the opposite end of the scale, all you need for a small garden is the simple bubble fountain on page 160. A bowl or reservoir of water is covered by a wire mesh, over which pebbles are placed, so that the water spouting over the pebbles falls back into the bowl to be recirculated.

I like to see water features made from unusual, but simple, objects – such as a really large pebble with a hole in it, through which the water can flow or a column made from machine-cut regular blocks of York stone. For a minimalist style, there is the flat ground-level feature in black (page 49). For a more dramatic effect, water can cascade down steps (above). Some designers use stainless steel or glass for modern water sculptures; others use really strong colours, see opposite top: a single spout through which air and water are mixed to give a frothy cascade.

Pages 42 115 121 ◀◀

HOT TUBS & SPAS can be installed on their own, in which case they can easily be designed to fit in with surrounding planting to provide screening. Alternatively they can be built in conjunction

with a swimming pool, perhaps at the side, although the bodies of water must be kept separate. Hot tubs come as round-shaped barrels in red cedar or other hardwood; heating can be built in under the tub. Essential is a surround that is pleasant to walk on, as with a swimming pool. A strong pump to power massaging water jets (using air pumps to aerate the water) is needed.

PONDS, especially still water, provide something I use wherever I can, as to me it gives an extra level of relaxation and tranquillity. Always use a black pond liner for the best reflections, and the larger the scale of the pond, the better the reflections will be (in any case, small pools often need movement, however slight, mainly to keep them fresh).

Often the most difficult decision regarding a pond, particularly a formal one with a regular shape, is the pond surround. Simple pavings, such as limestone blocks surrounded by white gravel (page 96), work best. For an informal pond, and where wildlife needs to be considered, pebbles will form a more natural perimeter.

Pages 45 96 ◀◀

RILLS & CHANNELS are narrow strips of still or moving water, often placed between two pools of water such as in Mogul garden designs (like the Taj Mahal in India or the Alhambra in Spain). A modern version of a rill could simply be formed from two panels of toughened glass running perhaps from a fountain feature at one end along 10 or 20m (30 or 60ft) to a pool.

Pages 63 65 ◀◀

A SWIMMING POOL in any garden has to be thought about carefully if it is not to appear like a blot on the landscape. A pool should be a feature in its own right and add something to the overall design of a garden. My pools tend to have straight edges; curves never fit neatly with the design. I also avoid raised swimming pools, which are usually cheaper, but to my mind if you cannot have a sunken one, do not bother at all. Sometimes a pool can be integrated into the natural slope of the garden, at least at one end.

An outdoor shower by the pool is one of the sexiest things to have in a garden – not only to wash off chlorine, but because showering in the open feels so good. When designing a swimming pool, you must always enclose it for safety reasons, and always get a professional to install it.

Pages 38 67 ◀◀

fountains & spouts

Even in the smallest garden a water feature adds something special: it looks refreshing, and the movement and noise of the flow should be soothing – just enough to mask other, less welcome sounds.
Clockwise, from top left:
These pieces of stone are drilled and fitted with a pipe, allowing water to bubble gently up through them and ripple down over a slab too shallow to call a pool; the blue fountain is altogether more classical, but painted a most vibrant colour to match the pool and surrounding walls; an old lead hopper is used as a reservoir for a spout into a pool constructed of glass blocks; tiny copper pipes drip water onto copper saucers balanced so that when they become full they tip with a magical, tinkling sound.

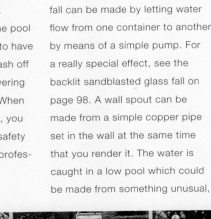

WATERFALLS & STEPS A basic fall can be made by letting water flow from one container to another by means of a simple pump. For a really special effect, see the backlit sandblasted glass fall on page 98. A wall spout can be made from a simple copper pipe set in the wall at the same time that you render it. The water is caught in a low pool which could be made from something unusual, such as a decorative metal tank or the glass brick container (see above); uplit at night, this gives a fantastic effect of ripples on the water surface.

The water steps (see opposite) are very contemporary, and when the sun is out they reflect like a series of mirrors. They require sloping or terraced ground. A single ramp is easier to line, using butyl liner; the steps are constructed over this, with a catchment tank at the bottom which conceals the pump. You need a good reservoir at the top for more powerful 'falls', and the supply needs to be topped up frequently because of evaporation. A strong pump is required, both to circulate the water and keep the reservoir in the tank full enough to enable the water to flow freely.

Pages 27 34 42 79 ◀◀

raised water features & tubs

Water features raised off the ground are well worth considering, as they are usually much easier to construct than a sunken pond which involves soil excavation and disposal.

From left to right:
This large pool in a purpose-built steel container is at ground level – it is glimpsed through a pergola constructed using steel rods, and the raised beds on the opposite side have a contrasting willow-weave texture; plate glass forms this suspended fish-tank (see also page 18); a small hot tub with timber panel surround and edge for sitting; short lengths of timber are again used but in a shallow, barrel-like construction, held by metal bands and with a metal rim; another view of the first pool shows it is one of a pair, with an angular construction and fountain.

DECORATIVE FINISHES & EDGINGS

BALLS or spheres in stone and marble have made a comeback, not just as a 'finale' on the top of brick or stone pillars, but in their own right, in rows on the ground or perhaps as a statement at the end of a pathway, or to define steps or corners. They have a practical use at ground level as they stop the hosepipe from wandering across flowerbeds and destroying plants. Transparent or coloured glass balls add a newer touch, perhaps to the top of an obelisk or decorative frame.
Pages 96 121 ◀◀

COPING gives a lovely clean effect to walls. It makes all the difference along the top of a rendered wall, either in cast concrete sections or, to look really fantastic, in limestone – what I call the Rolls Royce of coping! Most reconstituted stone companies have a good range of copings, but the lighter-coloured ones are more effective. Placing a timber coping along the edge of a galvanized or brick planter to match surrounding decking will make a nice link.
Page 92 ◀◀

EDGINGS & SOIL OR GRAVEL RETAINERS are used to hold back soil, gravel or bark chippings, or to give a definite boundary to a path or border, or emphasize a design. Simplest of all are white pebbles placed between planters and pavings (page 110). Edging stones can be made to a specific design from reconstituted stone and varied with a decorative relief, such as the half-artichoke motif

on page 112. Victorian edging stones, like those with a rolled top, look great placed next to a simple material like plain grey concrete paving. I also recommend plain concrete edges, as they are much cheaper. Metal strips can give a very crisp look (see page 100) and develop an attractive patina as they weather, while timber can look good painted or stained, but is not, of course, as long lasting.

FINIALS, to top a summerhouse or gazebo, formerly made in wood or black-painted wrought iron work, are nowadays often made by artists out of interesting metal alloys and used on all sorts of structures such as the top of fence posts. Finials are available in varied styles, such as the classic French ball finial or imperial obelisk.

GUTTERING, drainpipes and drain covers should, if possible, tie in with the look of the garden or at least not clash with it. If you move into a new house and need to replace them, the decision on their finish should only be made once you know what style the rest of the garden is going to be. In general metal looks more handsome than plastic, such as this galvanized finish. I also like using copper and alloy, which are much more commonly used in the US; and traditional cast iron looks very smart. For a quick makeover of jaded plastic guttering, I recommend painting with silver hammerite, as black can look so old-fashioned. I have also used clear glass for guttering along the exterior glass wall of a conservatory. Otherwise I prefer pipework to be painted in a similar colour to the walls of the building so that it almost disappears.

PEBBLES placed on-edge as a cosmetic ground dressing, such as between limestone paving and a large container (see below), or as a simple edging, are a lovely clean way to edge paths or beds, soften the look of pavings or hide pond liners. It may have started with my interest in Zen gardens and minimalism, but I then began to think of different ways to use them, such as combined with square mesh, or drilled with a hole and placed on a steel rod.
Pages 45 79 111 ◀◀

ROOF COVERINGS Sheds and outbuildings are often covered in unattractive materials. For a smarter, cleaner and not too rustic look, cover a small back extension or outhouse roof with black plastic netting and grow climbing plants over it. Or lay willow-weave panels on the roof to act as a cosmetic dressing and place small planters on it – the willow-weave will stop the planters from slipping off. Some more imaginative roof coverings have turf growing on them, such as at Alvar Aalto's Villa Mairea in Finland or the concert hall at the Grieg Museum, near Bergen in Norway. For a simple disguise of an asphalt roof, try using flattish pebbles held in place by metal grille.

retainers & edgings

Clockwise, from top left:
strips of steel with steel 'pegs'; a pebble edge 'finishes' steps and retains bark; slate, pebbles and turf form a series of edgings to gravel; a curved metal strip holds a lovely crescent bed; white pebbles set off a shiny container; low hazel hurdles reinforced by metal along a path.

After hard landscaping and planting, generally the third most important thing in your garden is the furniture, including recliners and umbrellas. In a small garden its visual impact means that it becomes part of the structure that holds a design together, so looks are really important. With seating, comfort rates just as highly as looks – it's no good having a great-looking bench that cost a lot of money if you hate sitting on it.

outside living

SEATS & TABLES

BUILT-IN SEATING works best as part of the garden's overall identity. The park bench above is one of a series of curving wood slatted seats with either concrete bases or metal frames (page 34). In the garden on pages 92–3, a bench runs along two whole sides of the garden. The bench is stone-clad and is teamed with a permanent stone-slab table (its base made of concrete), which gives a solid, lasting appearance.

On a terrace or roof garden, built-in timber benches with small slatted seats and backs along a perimeter edge, perhaps between planters, are space-saving and can also act as a balustrade.

Pages 121 130 ◄◄

DINING TABLES AND CHAIRS

The whole eating outside experience has at last taken the world by storm, and the major transition from indoors to outdoors is very much in evidence. I am now being asked by clients to recommend tables and chairs smart enough for informal dining in the kitchen that can double up for outside dining. Iroko is possibly the smartest of the hardwoods: a table and co-ordinating chairs with cushions in white or cream calico and matching cream canvas umbrella is hard to beat as an outside dining set; other woods such as Western red cedar are also smart, but remember to exercise caution in buying hardwoods (page 160).

If outside space for a table is limited, consider making a table top which is hinged to fold flat against a wall; it can double as a work surface.

Pages 72 121 128 138 144 ◄◄

FREE-STANDING SEATING

Generally, I prefer free-standing seating that can easily be moved around to create different layouts and identities. This is why I love metal chairs and tables, whether wrought iron, alloy or aluminium (see page 154). The really great alloy chairs on page 80, though they may not look it, are fabulously comfortable. Originally designed for prisons in America, they cannot be broken or damaged in any way. I use them for extra seating on my roof terrace. Some modern designs have alloy frames and wooden slatted or sandblasted glass seats. I have also seen good examples of square-topped air-conditioning pipes used as chairs, with a wooden seat added. Where budget is a concern, I don't think you can beat a classic deck chair, its fabric co-ordinated with your scheme (page 82), though folding canvas 'directors' chairs take up less space. The range of plastic chairs is improving, especially in colours other than white. (White is best suited to shaded areas, as it can be particularly dazzling in bright sunlight.) I also use wicker, plastic and even natural logs and driftwood for seating, as long as the design – and comfort factor – is right.

Pages 60 68 – 9 ◄◄

STORAGE

I often build storage space into garden seating, such as the high-backed seat (below left) with log-filled chambers on either side. Galvanized plates on top of the two columns protect the logs from getting wet. The slatted seat section lifts to reveal a storage box for tools etc. I recommend that barbecues are designed as part of the garden's furnishings, or at least have an outside cupboard where a free-standing barbecue can be quickly stowed away. Storage of rubbish is often a bit of a dilemma in urban environments. A free-standing unit or 'cupboard' with a planter on top is one sensible solution. I nearly always suggest simple galvanized dustbins, or alternatively that a dustbin storage area is built into the overall design, where the unit forms part of the boundary between neighbours. It has the shared fence built into it, and the roof is in galvanized sheeting to match nearby pots.

Hose storage can often be a problem: once I solved this by fixing a chrome inner of a car wheel to the wall; with a clear hose reeled around it, it makes an unusual feature.

Page 81 ◄◄

seating combinations

From left to right: The retaining wall doubles as a seating area around three sides, made of blockwork and clad in stone (the table is also built in); in a very small garden this bench seat and log store becomes the main focal point along the entrance wall; an L-shaped bench on two sides of this garden also acts as a balustrade in front of a basement swimming pool roof; here a seat with a powder-coated back is supported by galvanized steel planters (the seat is bolted to the metal using chrome fixings). The seat has a striped squab cushion to ensure comfort.

LIGHTING

style tips

Garden lighting is either for decoration or security, and it is always better to keep these functions separate. Getting the right decorative lighting is not easy, but use soft lighting to highlight certain key features, to create mystery, depth of field and illusions. Floodlit gardens always appear flat. Use coloured lighting only to light one area or a wall with a single colour, perhaps for a night-time effect that changes the mood of the garden completely.

DOWNLIGHTERS are particularly useful for highlighting features or flat surfaces, such as a sculpture of table, from above. I also use them suspended along the length of a planted pergola to create dappled pools of light. If placed higher, such as in a tree, their effect is more subtle and best appreciated from a distance: it looks rather like the moon shining through the branches. I love the effect of downlighting using a simple spotlight with a narrow beam for outside dining tables.

FIBRE OPTICS is quite a new lighting idea, and works from a single source, which sends light through strands of glass fibre, to make small individual light points (see page 17 and detail, page 172 far right). It can also look wonderful fitted into a water stairway, as on page 166.

FLOODLIGHTS I use floodlights as security lights, with a sensor system. They are activated once a beam has been broken by an intruder, once all other lights are turned off. I will occasionally floodlight a garage area, or use it to make a spectacle out of a large tree or other feature that is some distance from the house.

LOW-TECH LIGHTING I use candles outdoors whenever possible. Using glass shades stops the wind blowing them out and magnifies their light. I use a series of large outdoor candles to light pathways or form a ring of light around topiary trees; these have special metal tops to protect the flame. Flares on bamboo poles provide dramatic welcome for a party; the poles hold a metal can with a wick, which is filled with paraffin – lovely in winter. I like to use festoon lighting either at Christmas-time, or as lighting for serving tables at a summer barbecue. I prefer using white bulbs only, but soft colours are all right as long as they are not mixed. I often use pea lights to outline the shape of a feature tree, especially at Christmas, or especially in a pair of clear-stemmed trees at either side of an entrance.

NEON LIGHTING always requires installation by a professional as it entails various health and safety regulations (if tubes are broken, they can give off noxious gases). Lamps come in many different colours to produce a whole range of effects and images; I like to use neon to give a sharp line of light and also strong colour to a particular occasion.
Page **172** ◀◀

POST LIGHTS, ideal for lighting pathways, come in many styles, but I like the ones with cleanest lines, perhaps just a timber upright and metal grille top, approximately 1m (3ft) tall. Plain black or metal 'mushroom' lights set low along a driveway can also look great.

SAFETY LIGHTING Certain parts of the garden that could be a danger, not just to the young and

171

wall lights

Wall-mounted lights come in many styles, from ornate coach lamps to low-key modern fittings as general illumination for a patio, side path or front door. They can be disguised as recessed fittings, hiding the light source or, as here, form a feature in themselves. *From left to right*: black was chosen for this fitting, to match the black-painted window frames and doors of the house; one of a series of six down-lights in a conservatory, activated by the cable strung on either side; this custom-made light, a galvanized steel box, has a detachable wire guard and takes either a 60W incandescent lamp or a less powerful 18W compact fluorescent lamp; switches and safety cable housings made from shower piping can form an attractive feature in their own right; a domed light with opaque glass in galvanized casing and safety trunking for the cable.

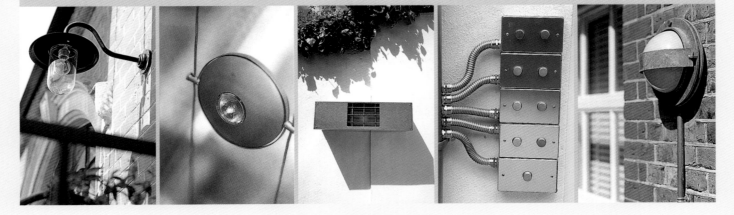

old but even the sure footed, should be lit. Pools are one example, but steps are another that it's easy to overlook.

Recessed brick lights in clear glass, the same size as a brick and so flush with the wall, are ideal for a flight of steps, or along the brick edging of a pathway, and are easily built in. Uplighters should have a lockable installation sleeve for safety with children.

SECURITY LIGHTING A must within any garden, especially in areas very close to the house. I always advise that the security lighting is on a separate circuit, which can be overridden if need be, as the security lighting should be on a sensor, to alert you to intruders when the main garden lighting is not on.

172

Never rely on your security lights to be your main form of decorative lighting, as the fittings are usually much larger than standard or low-voltage ones, and they give a flat, bright, appearance to a garden, and lack mood or character.

mood lighting

As darkness falls, create a special atmosphere: *clockwise, from top left*: This galvanized light gives a soft glow through a sandblasted glass panel; multiple reflections from this blue neon lighting; white perspex light cover; the whole of this roof terrace is uplit from fittings in the wood floor, creating shadow-play through the plants; candle-light, the most subtle of all; a great example of a design using fibre optics (see also page 17); detail of the roof terrace uplighting; detail of candle light; light across pebbles seen through lionweld kennedy floor grid.

SPOTLIGHTS These are good for featuring a specimen tree, statue or urn on a plinth, a piece of modern sculpture, or a small pond or other water feature, as they can be tilted in any direction. They are either fixed to a wall bracket or can be movable, attached to a

short metal spike pushed into the ground and moved at will according to cable length. They come in a black, white or polished metal finish (other colours to order), to take a 50W or 75W halogen lamp and can be supplied with clear or frosted glass.

UNDERWATER LIGHTING A good selection of fittings is available from the simplest, that throw a single beam of light through a pool, to high-tech fittings for back-lighting and that change the colour of the water. For the water feature on pages 98 and 105, a custom-made light was used. In

the pool itself are three under-water uplighters trained on the sand-blasted glass waterfall, to cast a rippling, dance-like effect over the surface of the water.

UPLIGHTERS will create good shadow effects when set at the base of a wall with plants growing up it or beneath a shrub or tree, so that the undersides of the branches and leaves are uplit. Floor-mounted light fittings are usually stainless steel with tough-ened glass, recessed ones are ideal for roof terraces or paths. They have a fixed beam or can be directional. Some are designed to perform in extreme environments; some fittings take low-voltage, fluorescent or cluster lamps.

mains versus low voltage lighting

Low-voltage lighting is fast overtaking mains voltage for smaller gardens, mainly because the smaller fittings (half the size of mains) are easier to conceal, and low voltage is suitable where short cable runs are required. Only when lighting large gardens and large trees and shrubs do you have to use the mains voltage system. Firstly, from a safety point of view, mains voltage should be plastic-coated armoured cable, and should be buried at least 45cm (18in) under the soil. Special outdoor sockets are a must. I would always recommend a master switch in the house or other convenient place, and having separate systems for different parts of the garden which can be controlled by a remote control. I also recommend using a lighting specialist when fitting outdoor lighting.

SOFT FURNISHINGS

recline to relax

A hammock strung between two trees always seems the ultimate form of relaxation on a hot day – but not many gardens have two trees, let alone in exactly the right place to be of use. Here the support poles are steel uprights, set into concrete and then – the clever bit – slender conifers have been planted to disguise the steel. The pool loungers are the ultimate in cool elegance; made of slatted timbers with the plainest of fabric covers.

Pages `78` `84` `138` ◀◀

AWNINGS, as well as protecting the interior from sunlight, allow you to make fuller use of the garden; they can be an excellent way of extending the house for a temporary event, making a cosy, enclosed space for dining outside, with protection from the midday sun or a shower of rain. Again white or cream look best (see above), but for more drama try using yellow. They will need spring cleaning with soapy water and you may need to replace the fabric every three or four years. Black frames are the most versatile for matching with surroundings. Awnings are expensive to install, and the need for maintenance will depend on their exposure to sun and weather, as well as situation.
Page `84` ◀◀

BLINDS For conservatories, which are often as much garden structure as part of the house,

blinds are nearly always needed to prevent them heating up too much, especially when they contain plants. These, as well as outside awnings, will affect the overall look of that part of the garden and so they should be selected with this in mind. When choosing from the various options on the market, remember that simple white or off-white fabrics are best at deflecting the sun and always look good. If interior blinds cannot be fitted, exterior blinds are available, e.g. in aluminium.

HAMMOCKS The traditional 'sailors' sleeping hammock always seems like the ideal relaxation for a hot, sultry day in the garden but it's not always easy to find the right place to hang it. 'Sitting' hammocks, which are hung from a single hook or branch of a tree, are becoming popular in India and can sometimes be found in ethnic

catalogues. String is the usual material for this type of hammock, with plain wood supports to hold the sides apart. The most durable material for reclining hammocks is heavy-duty canvas (above right).

UMBRELLAS are available in many different sizes from the cheapest coloured canvas type used for the beach, to a more sophisticated version that might be some 5m (16ft) square; four of

them placed together would be an alternative to a marquee for a largish gathering. Umbrellas can be custom-made to co-ordinate with plant-colour themes, such as orange with a blue-and-orange planting scheme, or red. To keep an umbrella stable the best type of stand is one (or more, so that you can change them about) permanent holes 15cm (6in) deep in a lump of concrete set in the ground.
Page `53` ◀◀

173

screens and shades

Creating divisions can be done in many more ways than using hedges or trellis – why not use plain canvas or simple mesh like this gauzy material (*right above*) to screen off an area or simply to add a sense of mystery for a party? Equally, though an umbrella is the traditional way to create shade, and this orange one (*right*) has a really strong impact, some light, gauzy material is a lovely way to make an awning; it greatly increases the sense of relaxation and comfort in the swimming pool area (*far right*).

A successful garden has the right mix of plants, chosen to complement buildings and other hard materials, as well as for their structure, texture, colour and scent. The most architectural are the feature plants used either singly or in groups; others are there for a more supporting role, as backdrop, edging or groundcover. All have their part to play in any strong design. (All are hardy in cooler climates unless stated otherwise.)

<u>100 key plants</u>

ARCHITECTURAL & ACCENT PLANTS

These are the plants to help you achieve a strong identity in your garden – that stand out in a border, 'hold' a planting scheme, or form a centrepiece in a paved area.

<u>ACANTHUS SPINOSUS</u> This perennial has dramatic, glossy green, deeply cut, spiked arching leaves and striking spires of white flowers with purple bracts borne in late summer, which dry well for decorating in the home. It grows to 1.2m (4ft) high in well-drained soil and a sunny position, but tolerates some shade. The crowns will need protection in the first winter after planting, in colder areas.

<u>AGAVE AMERICANA</u> (century plant) Bold, silvery grey-green, fleshy leaves, which unfurl slowly create a very structural plant of 1-2m (3-6ft). Some varieties are hardy in temperate regions but others, especially variegated types like this *A.a.* 'Marginata', will need winter protection. It needs well-drained soil; good for a sunny terrace or conservatory.
Page 131 ◀◀

<u>ASPLENIUM SCOLOPENDRIUM</u> (hart's tongue fern) With wonderfully wandering strap-like, glossy green fronds reaching 60cm (2ft) long at times, this is a useful perennial for damp, shady places. It tolerates acid but loves alkaline soil. *A.s.* 'Crispum' has wavy-edged leaves.

<u>ASTELIA CHATAMICA</u> 'Silver Spear' Its arching, leathery, sword-like leaves in silver-grey grow to 1.2m (4ft) long and tolerate a sunny or shady position.

<u>BRAHEA ARMATA</u> (blue hesper palm, blue-fan palm) A single-stemmed plant with silvery blue-grey, large palm-shaped leaves, 1-3m (3-10ft) across, growing on stalks. In summer in warm areas it has panicles of yellow flowers. This stately plant looks great underplanted with *Senecio cineraria* (see page 160) and is frost tender.
Page 130 ◀◀

<u>CANNA INDICA & CANNA</u> hybrids Tropical in appearance, with slender stems and glamorous dark-green leaves, these plants can grow anywhere between 60cm (2ft) and 1.5m (5ft) in height, with flowering stems in red, orangey-red or golden-yellow. I always think that this needs to be planted in groups of five or more to gain maximum effect, in sheltered positions and fertile soil in full sun.

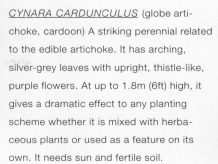

<u>CYNARA CARDUNCULUS</u> (globe artichoke, cardoon) A striking perennial related to the edible artichoke. It has arching, silver-grey leaves with upright, thistle-like, purple flowers. At up to 1.8m (6ft) high, it gives a dramatic effect to any planting scheme whether it is mixed with herbaceous plants or used as a feature on its own. It needs sun and fertile soil.

<u>ERYNGIUM GIGANTEUM</u> A real favourite for its bold, silver-green flower clusters. A biennial, it self-seeds quite easily – I love it because it pops up in odd places every year. I like to grow it near *Festuca glauca* and *Perovskia* 'Blue Spire'; here *E.g.* 'Silver Ghost' is complemented by the yellow heads of santolina and feathery artemisia leaves. *E. alpinum is smaller and* has lilac-blue bracts and flowers.

<u>FATSIA JAPONICA</u> (Japanese aralia syn. *Aralia japonica)* A great structural plant because of its lovely palm-like, dense glossy green leaves and height – it grows to an impressive 3m (10ft) tall. It has clusters of tiny white flowers in autumn followed by black, berry-like fruits. It needs fertile soil, tolerates sun or shade and is frost hardy, but may need protection from strong winds.

<u>FOENICULUM VULGARE</u> 'Purpureum' (bronze fennel) Its lovely feathery, aromatic foliage is purple-bronze when young and makes a striking background for many other plants, both enhancing and contrasting with a range of colours. The yellow-ochre flower-heads appear in late summer. It loves full sun and fertile, well-drained soil and can reach 2m (6ft) in height. The stems stay looking architectural through the winter.

<u>MISCANTHUS SINENSIS</u> This species of bold deciduous grasses contains a host of different varieties from 1m (3ft) to 4m (12ft) high, in lovely, bold, arching clumps of bright green or lighter, variegated or blue-green leaves. With dense, silky, silvery or reddish panicles (see page 182), they are particularly good in autumn and on into winter; the plumes are best left until new growth appears in spring, when all stems should be cut back. *M.s.* 'Silberturm' and ' Silberfeder'('Silver Feather') are good tall grasses; *M.s.* 'Nippon' is smaller and turns copper-brown.

<u>ONOPORDUM ACANTHIUM</u> This has to be in my top five structural plants, not only for its leaf texture with silvery-grey, furry, almost webbed-type leaves, which are very imposing when introduced to a planting scheme, but also for its erect stems, which can reach 3m (10ft) in height bearing thistle-like, pale purple flowerheads on spiky bracts. Once introduced, you may find this biennial self-seeding around different parts of your garden. Grow in fertile, well-drained soil in full sun.

PHORMIUM (New Zealand or mountain flax) A great architectural evergreen up to 1.5m (5ft) high with distinctive, sword-like leaves which grow into bold clumps. It loves moist, fertile, well-drained soil in full sun and needs protection from frost. The two species (P. cookianuam and P. tenax) vary from bright green (page 73) to bronze-purple-leaved (P. tenax 'Dazzler', page 55) and variegated cream, green and pink-margined (P. cookianum subsp. hookeri 'Tricolor'). **Pages 7 55 60 ◀◀**

PHYLLOSTACHYS sp. (bamboo) Whether used as a single specimen or as a screen to help disguise a neighbour's garden, bamboo is a great asset. Originating from East Asia and the Himalayas, these evergreen bamboos can be great spreaders, and reach some 5m (16ft) in height, but in cooler climates will stay as more compact clumps. Some keep their green colouring, older leaves of others turn more yellowy. The black-stemmed species P. nigra, with masses of oblong, mid-green leaves, looks good underplanted with the black 'grass', Ophiopogon planiscapus 'Nigrescens' or in soil top-dressed with grey pebbles. **Pages 76 105 ◀◀**

YUCCA FILAMENTOSA (yucca) These plants make great impact planted in groups of three or more. Though not so hardy as the species, Y.f. 'Variegata' with its striped stems is worth having as a single feature plant. Its strap-like leaves are 75cm (30in) long, and its occasional, upright flower spikes to 2m (6ft) high bear whitish panicles. **Page 50 ◀◀**

cacti & succulents

Whole cactus gardens make stylish architectural plantings of their own, as with these contrasting spheres and columns (left), but also create structure in an informal planting (right). Here they are grouped with a large bromeliad, Puya berteroniana, which unlike the cacti has sprays of grass-like leaves.

FEATURE TREES & SHRUBS

These I have chosen on individual merit — for fine form or colour, or both. Many trees can be restricted in their growth by judicious pruning and also by being grown in a large container.

ACACIA DEALBATA (mimosa) A half-hardy tree from Australasia with lovely soft, ferny leaves. It must be grown in a sheltered location (such as an inner city courtyard) and can reach a height of 8m (25ft) plus. When in blossom, it is covered with long racemes of the most heavenly scented, fluffy yellow flowers.

ACER sp. (maple) A very large group of trees and shrubs, with quite distinctive leaf forms. A. palmatum is a good, slow-growing maple, which containerizes well (page 92), It has lovely deep-cut leaves turning to fiery reddish-orange in autumn. A.p. dissectum is one of the most decorative, with its serrated leaf and autumn colour. A. griseum has glossy, mahogany-coloured bark.

BETULA UTILIS var. jacquemontii (Himalayan birch) A most wonderful feature tree because of its dazzling, silvery-white bark (see picture, top), which has a peeling effect. It can eventually grow to quite a size so be careful to choose the right location. It is extremely hardy. **Page 128 – 9 ◀◀**

CEDRUS DEODARA A majestic evergreen tree which has to be one of my favourite conifers mostly because of its slightly weeping habit with its soft, grey-blue needles. It can grow to 15m (50ft) but will remain small if restricted in a large container. **Page 93 ◀◀**

CONITHUS ARBOREUS A lovely evergreen tree, which can grow to 4m (12ft) in height but can also be wall-trained; it bears lovely panicles of pale blue flowers in summer. This is a good, fast-growing variety.

CORYLUS sp. (hazel) The purple hazel, C. maxima 'Purpurea', is a striking feature plant either set among other shrubs or as a setting for herbaceous plants, with quite an upright habit. It can grow to 5m (16ft). C. avellana 'Contorta' is the corkscrew hazel. **Pages 116 ◀◀**

COTINUS COGGYGRIA 'Royal Purple' (smoke bush) Another lovely purple foliage plant and, with its rounded leaves and fluffy plume-like flowers, it looks good amongst herbaceous plants or as a feature plant within a shrub border. It favours a sunny position and, like other cotinus, will give superb autumn colour. It responds well to hard pruning.

CUPRESSUS SEMPERVIRENS (Italian cypress) This has a distinctive, upright habit and aroma on a warm, sunny day. Its long, slender appearance (it will grow to15m/50ft) evokes the atmosphere of the Mediterranean landscape. *Juniperus scopulorum* 'Skyrocket' is a good alternative junior tree for a small garden or container. **Page 138** ◀◀

DICKSONIA ANTARCTICA (soft or woolly tree fern) This is rapidly becoming a keen favourite in urban gardens with its wonderful trunk and lush, spreading, fern-like canopy. It is frost tender and needs winter protection in all temperate climates, but can do well in sheltered city micro-climates. It is certainly not a cheap option to buy, but can grow to a height of 4-5m (12-16ft).

EUCALYPTUS GLAUCESENS (Tingiringi gum) This is an excellent variety because of its whitish bark and bluish leaves: the young foliage has rounded blue-white leaves (page 112) which turn to slender, pointed blue-grey adult leaves. Eucalyptus can be a nuisance as they are deep-rooted and grow to 12m (40ft) if not kept in check. They need sun and shelter from cold winds.

FICUS CARICA (common fig) This small, shrubby deciduous tree, long grown in Europe for its fruits, feels right for the contemporary minimalist garden with its simple shape and greenish-grey leaves, together with its 'primitive' fruit. Reaches about 3m (10ft) in height and so is ideal for smaller gardens. Grow in full sun or partial shade. **Page 78** ◀◀

HAMAMELIS MOLLIS (Chinese witch hazel) A distinctive winter-flowering upright shrub, as its yellow flower clusters like crinkled ribbon (and with a scent second to none) are borne on the bare stems. Another bonus is its great autumn colour. *H.* x *intermedia* is a cross with Japanese witch hazel and has yellow, dark red or orange flowers; 'Jelena' has wonderful copper-orange flowers. Witch hazels grow to 4m (12ft), flourish in sun or semi-shade and are not particularly fussy about soil.

LIQUIDAMBAR STYRACIFLUA (sweet gum) A slow-growing deciduous tree with an upright, dome-shaped habit, and well-worth having as a feature tree for its amazing autumn colours in red, orange and purple. It does eventually grow large (25m/80ft), so make sure you have the space for it. It favours a sunny position.

NERIUM OLEANDER (rose bay) This shrub or small tree (2-6m/6-20ft tall) has fine, lance-shaped, leathery leaves and is known for its fragrant pink flowers, although there are white-flowered varieties. It will grow well in a sheltered spot but is not frost hardy.

NYSSA SYLVATICA A distinctive, pyramid-shaped tree for a large garden (it grows to some 20m/70ft), which has astounding bright orange and red leaf colour in autumn. **Page 178** ◀◀

OLEA EUROPAEA (common olive) This is the plant that I couldn't live without because it has all the major qualities that an evergreen should have: lovely silver-grey leaves (grey-green above and silvery beneath) – the new growth is always pretty to see; excellent form (the young trees are flame-shaped); and, in more mature specimens, great character – with their knotted bark. Needs shelter in frost-prone areas. **Pages 63 80** ◀◀

PARROTIA PERSICA A great tree with a wide habit, and which is slow growing and has the most intense autumn colour of orange and red (page 178), and an interesting winter flower not dissimilar in appearance to *Hamamelis mollis* flowers, but coloured red, like stamens.

PHOENIX CANARIENSIS (Canary Island date palm) Lovely for its elegant fronds; with its broad, columnar trunk with oblong, horizontal markings, it can grow to some 15m (50ft). A good palm for frost-free areas including city micro-climates. **Page 65** ◀◀

PINUS RADIATA (Monterey pine) Eventually large but narrow-growing, domed tree with lovely bright, darkish green needles and yellow-brown cones (female tree). It tolerates seaside salty air and so makes a good windbreak. *P. pinea*, the umbrella pine, has radiating branches, young glaucous-blue needles and eventually a wonderful flat top. It is grown a lot in the Mediterranean area and is a 'must' if you want to recreate that atmosphere. **Pages 75 81** ◀◀

PYRUS SALICIFOLIA 'Pendula' (weeping pear) A spreading ornamental tree with bright, silver-grey, willow-like foliage which shapes well, making this a good tree for smaller gardens; it can even be clipped to form low hedging. It has creamy-white flowers in spring and will reach a height of 8m (25ft). Grow in full sun or part-shade, in good soil.

directory

QUERCUS ILEX (Holm oak) This wonderful, slow-growing evergreen can be containerized for a small garden or even a roof space (page 139). It has fine, silver-grey leaves when young (it is not unlike an olive but much hardier), and can be trained as topiary.

Page 145 ◀◀

SALIX sp. (willow) The slender stems can easily be trained to form lattice fencing and screen, using minimal support (see page 45). *S. alba* var. *sericea* (silver willow) is a beautiful silvery, narrow-leaved tree with a slightly rounded habit; it has a lovely shimmer in the wind, and forms a good backdrop to a mixed shrub border, or stands on its own as a striking feature tree. (page 108). *S. exigua* (page 108) is extremely hardy, and like all willows, responds well to cutting back and prefers moist soil.

SORBUS ARIA 'Lutescens' (whitebeam) In early spring you can't beat the wonderful silvery-grey leaves of this lovely tree, which are shortly followed by creamy, off-white flowers. The leaves turn dark green after fruiting, followed by lovely golden-yellow autumnal foliage. Height to 10m (30ft) or more.

VIBURNUM OPULUS (guelder rose) This bushy, deciduous viburnum has an almost maple-shaped leaf with vivid autumn colour, but also lovely spheres of acid-green turning to white flowers, not dissimilar to hydrangea heads, in spring, which are followed by yellow or red berries. Left to itself it will grow to 5m (16ft).

178

STRUCTURE & BACKBONE PLANTING

These plants, though not all evergreen, make good soft structures or backdrops to borders. They are all amenable to clipping into hedges, edgings or topiary features.

BUXUS SEMPERVIRENS (common box) This brilliant, small-leaved evergreen has been used successfully for centuries as an edging plant, grown to about 30cm (12in) high, as it responds so well to clipping. It is often used as hedging or clipped topiary, such as cones and spirals; being relatively slow-growing, it holds it shape well. Box can grow to 5m (16ft) to make a superb focal tree. It prefers a sunny or lightly shaded position and is easy to grow from cuttings. *B.s.* 'Suffruticosa' is a dwarf form, suitable for really low 15cm (6in) edging. *B. microphylla* has smaller, darker leaves.

Pages 30 59 71 85 105 143 ◀◀

CARPINUS BETULUS (hornbeam) This has a smaller, toothed leaf, very similar to beech but faster-growing and forms a topiary shape or hedge quickly. It is reasonably hardy, loves full sun and tends to have hop-like fruits in the autumn; it hangs onto its brown leaves during the winter, giving wind protection to other plants in its vicinity.

Pages 28 – 9 41 ◀◀

good autumn foliage

Clockwise, from top left, berries and foliage of *Viburnum opulus*; leaves of *Parrotia persica*; *Acer palmatum*; *Nyssa sylvatica*.

Others to plant for autumn colour are: *Berberis thunbergii* f. *atropurpurea* and *B.t.* 'Rose Glow'; *Cotinus coggygria* 'Royal Purple'; *Hamamelis mollis* and *Liquidambar styraciflua* (page 177) and *Sorbus aria* 'Lutescens'.

ELAEAGNUS sp. The whole elaeagnus family make wonderful evergreen shrubs which are all very striking, including *E. pungens* 'Maculata' (left), a lovely golden-variegated form.

Although deciduous, the oleaster *E. angustifolia* 'Quicksilver' is one of the most striking silver varieties, with creamy-white, scented flowers in the summer on brownish stems. *E.* x *ebbingei* has paler green leaves.

All elaeagnus are good in exposed areas including coastal gardens.

FAGUS SYLVATICA (beech) With lovely fresh-green leaves in spring and amazing golden-yellow leaves in autumn, beech makes a substantial, thick hedge. Also a fabulous feature tree for a large garden (it matures to 25m / 80ft), especially *F.s.* f. *purpurea*, the copper beech, with its wonderful shiny purple-red leaves.

HEBE VERNICOSA (hebe) Small and compact (to 60cm/2ft), this is a great plant for edging borders with its lovely, dense green foliage (it has an architectural feel) and white flowers. It will tolerate dry soil and is an alternative to boxwood.

HEDERA HELIX (ivy) These most useful plants can be trained over walls, railings or along wires, and smaller-leaved varieties can be trained into topiary shapes over a wire frame, while the self-clinging varieties soon disguise walls (see opposite, with box balls). The lighter or variegated forms need sun (there is even a yellow form, 'Buttercup'), but the dark green, glossy-leaved forms do much to brighten a dark corner.
Pages 29 85 98 157 ◀◀

ILEX AQUIFOLIUM (holly) A very robust evergreen that makes excellent security hedging or a good backdrop, a feature tree, or clipped into topiary shapes, especially the variegated forms. Female plants (grown near a male plant) bear lovely red or yellow berries. *I. perado* subsp. *platyphylla* has broader leaves. Variegated forms need full sun, and all like a fairly moist soil.

LAURUS NOBILIS (bay laurel) A must in any size of garden as it can easily be cut to a cone or other topiary shape and its leaves have great and ancient culinary value. *L.n.* 'Aurea' has green and gold foliage. This plant likes a sheltered position as it is not altogether hardy, but does well in sun or shade.

LIGUSTRUM sp. (privet) With its evergreen, oval-shaped leaves, traditionally used as low hedging, it is excellent worked as topiary and it is a good substitute for boxwood, being a little more affordable. Here it is grown as a mophead ball on a stem. *L. delavayanum* has tiny leaves, which are good for intricate shapes; there is also a variegated form, *L. ovalifolium*.

Pages 40 80 ◀◀

hedge topiary

Hedging in flowing, organic shapes is much used in contemporary garden design in Continental Europe, both as an art form and to provide garden rooms and sheltered places for sitting or sunbathing. It can also be used to manipulate the feeling of depth, as in the garden at Parc André Citroen, Paris, (pages 28-9).

The curving forms shown below are from designer and nurseryman Piet Oudolf's garden at Hummelo in the Netherlands. Against a backdrop of tall trees, they provide a wonderfully stylish, formal stage set to the mainly informal planting of contrasting greens and russet-pink grasses.

MAGNOLIA GRANDIFLORA Once grown as a wall shrub, it is now often grown as a pyramid-shaped tree as it topiarizes easily (these regimented forms stand in a formal water feature at Parc André Citroen, page 165). It has glossy evergreen, 20cm (8in) long leaves with suede-like undersides and enormous 25cm (10in) across, cup-like, cream or pale yellow scented flowers.

PRUNUS LUSITANICA (laurel) Although not as popular as it used to be, laurel nevertheless provides a lovely, thick, quite fast-growing hedge that is relatively inexpensive. It has racemes of white, cup-shaped, scented flowers and pointed, glossy leaves. It looks best hand-pruned.

TAXUS BACCATA (English yew) Often grown as a hedge, or to stand alone as a specimen tree or as clipped topiary (see cloud yew, page 100); because of its dense, dark green foliage, it acts as the classic backdrop to other plants, foliage or flowers. Yew will grow in light shade, like underplanting in deciduous woodland.
Page 41 ◀◀

VIBURNUM TINUS (laurustinus) With a mounded habit of lovely glossy, green, oval-shaped leaves, it responds well to shaping and can be used as a hedging plant. The stems are ideal for winter flower arrangements, as are the clusters of white flowers that appear from late autumn to early spring. See also *V. opulus*. Page 178 ◀◀

FLOWERS & FOLIAGES

Here follows my recommended selection of smaller plants – flowers, grasses and foliage – for colour and scent, all of which contribute to the rich texture of the garden.

greens, blue-greys and silver

ALCHEMILLA MOLLIS (alchemilla, ladies' mantle) You cannot think of having a garden without including this gem of a plant, one of the best perennials, with lovely felt-like green leaves like fabric rosettes, and acid-green spikes of fluffy flowers. It works well in block plantings or as an edging plant, goes with any colour scheme and grows to about 45cm (18in) high.

ARTEMISIA 'Powis Castle' (wormwood) The lovely silver-filigree texture makes this aromatic plant an invaluable foliage feature; planted in drifts it is an excellent foil to intense flower colour. It grows to about 60cm (2ft) high with a good spread. Artemisias are Mediterranean plants and need a sunny, well-drained site.
Pages 85 121 ◀◀

BALLOTTA PSEUDODICTAMNUS Lovely pale green, rounded, cupped leaves form a mound to 45cm (18in) high. This plant needs poor, dry soil and full sun. With its silver-white young foliage, B. acetabulosa is a useful mat-forming and trailing plant, good as underplanting in containers.

BRACHYGLOTTIS sp. (syn. Senecio greyi) These shrubby plants, originally from New Zealand, have graphic leaf shapes with silver-white edges and are most useful mound-forming shrubs, either as part of a green and silver scheme, or as here, intermingled with other planting and colours, such as this pink geranium. They reach 2m (6ft) or more and make useful hedging and windbreaks as they respond well to clipping.

EUPHORBIA sp. (spurge) These showy plants are a must in whatever size of garden. E. charachias ssp. wulfenii is evergreen with structural, silvery grey-green leaves produced one year and very strong acid-green flowers, up to 1m (3ft) high, the following spring. E.c. ssp. characias is similar, but with deep purple-centred flowers. E. polychroma (shown below left, with ballotta) is smaller with acid-yellow flowers. Euphorbias tolerate various light levels and most are hardy.

FESTUCA GLAUCA (blue fescue) This grass forms an attractive tuft of straight, thin grey-blue leaves and looks best planted in groups of three or more, or en masse in sharp drifts. It grows 45cm (18in) tall and wide, in well-drained, not too fertile soil in full sun.
Page 73 ◀◀

HELLEBORUS FOETIDUS see H. orientalis **Page 182 ◀◀**

HELICHRYSUM ITALICUM (syn. H. angustifolium) An aromatic plant rather similar to artemisia with its silvery green, spiky leaves and clusters of yellow flowers. H.i. ssp. serotinum, known as the curry plant, is more compact and clips well to shape, and is good for edging. H. petiolare is a trailing plant with rounded leaves, good for underplanting in containers.

HOSTA sp. These wonderful clump-forming plants have exceptionally fine, sculptural leaf shapes and range in colour through pale green and cream variegated, bright emerald green and greenish-gold to bluish-grey. H. 'Halcyon' (left) has one of the finest, pointed leaf shapes. Pink or purple flowers are borne on racemes in summer. Hostas make excellent ground cover, planted in groups of five or more. Height varies from 25cm (10in) (H. 'Hadspen Blue') to a majestic 1m (3ft) or more (H. sieboldiana). They grow best in partial shade in moist soil.

PACHYSANDRA TERMINALIS A useful, low-growing, ground cover in that it tolerates low light levels and grows in all but the driest soils, spreading freely (see page 104-5, where it is used as underplanting to bamboo). Its dark green, glossy leaf clusters bear tiny white flowers in early summer. P.t. 'Variegata' has leaves with light margins.

PLEIOBLASTUS VARIEGATUS (syn. Arundinaria variegata) A super bamboo with a grass-like appearance and dark green, creamy-white variegated leaves on short stems. It grows to 45cm (18in) high and needs full sun and a moist, fertile soil. Plant in blocks to great effect.

ROSMARINUS OFFICINALIS (rosemary) Aromatic, upright, shrubby evergreen herb with pale or bright blue, purple-blue or white flowers, sometimes in early spring or into summer; some varieties flower again in autumn. Good in a border, against a sunny wall or as edging. Maximum height 1.5m (5ft).
Pages 52 181 ◀◀

SALVIA OFFICINALIS 'Purpurascens' (purple sage) One among many hundreds of shrubby sages, this variety has purple-red young leaves (page 40) and lilac-blue flowers, and grows to 45cm (18in). *S.o.* 'Tricolor' is cream-and-green variegated with pink margins to the young leaf-growth. All sages like sun and a light but moist, well-drained soil.

SANTOLINA CHAMAECYPARISSUS (cotton lavender, syn. *S. incana*) A very old established plant which has been used for many centuries; it forms a rounded shrub of dense, finely divided, oblong, greenish-grey leaves. It is good as an edging plant, to 50cm (20in) tall: the small, lemon-yellow, rounded flowerheads that form in summer can be removed as the plant is kept clipped into neat mounds. It likes sun and moderately fertile soil. **Pages 56-7 68** ◀◀

SENECIO CINERARIA (cineraria, syn. *Cineraria maritima*) It is usually grown as an annual for containers or bedding as its felt-like, bright silver-white leaves make great underplanting (see page 160). The yellow flowerheads which appear in summer are usually cut off.

STACHYS BYZANTINA (lamb's ears) A woolly, whitish-grey-leaved perennial that produces upright stems bearing small purple-pink flowers in summer, to 30cm (12in) or more high. *S.b.* 'Big Ears' has large, beautifully shaped, soft bluish-grey leaves that associate well with the pinks and purples of lavenders or rosemary. It likes full sun and a well-drained soil.

some recommended planting groups

A few fail-safe planting combinations that I recommend for planting in blocks of 3, 5 or 7, depending on space and size:

Artemisia 'Powis Castle' with *Sedum* 'Autumn Joy' and purple-flowered *Astrantia major*

White or blue delphinium with blocks of rue (*Ruta graveolens*) and *Lavandula angustifolia* 'Hidcote'

Anchusa azurea 'Loddon Royalist' with the Californian poppy (*Eschscholzia californica*) and French marigolds (*Tagetes*)

The giant tobacco plant (*Nicotiana sylvestris*) with white delphinium and *Santolina chamaecyparissus*.

The giant ornamental thistle (*Erygium giganteum*), the bluish-green grass *Festuca glauca* and spikes of *Perovskia* 'Blue Spire'.

cool blues, purples & black

AGAPANTHUS HYBRIDS These are lovely bright or dark blue, tubular-shaped flowers with round heads on long stems, which look good either used as architecture in a border, or grown in a handsome container. They range in height from 60 to150cm (2 – 5ft). *A.* 'Bressingham Hybrid' is a smaller, white form, to 90cm (3ft). They need full sun and fertile soil.

ANCHUSA AZUREA 'Loddon Royalist' (syn. *A. italica*) This plant is the deepest, brightest blue of any plant available. Its special clarity stands out well among silver or grey-leaved plants, or for great drama, plant the Californian poppy (*Eschscholzia californica*) next to it. It grows to 90-150cm (3–5ft) and unlike some less sturdy anchusas, does not need staking.

HEUCHERA MICRANTHA var. DIVERSIFOLIA 'Palace Purple' Shiny, deep purple foliage in spreading clumps makes this variety an excellent plant as an edging to contrast with paved walkways, or for block planting against 'hot' flower colours. It has delicate panicles of flowers in pale to bright pink in early summer. Grow in sun or shade in fertile, moist but well-drained soil.

LAVANDULA ANGUSTIFOLIA 'Hidcote' Though the species lavender is best for scent, this variety has the deepest purple flower spikes of all the lavenders, with silvery grey foliage and a neater form. It makes a great edging plant or is stunning as block planting. French lavender, *L. stoechas*, is a bushier shrub in purple, pink or white varieties. **Page 111** ◀◀

MECONOPSIS BETONICIFOILIA (Himalayan or Tibetan blue poppy) This large poppy (to 1.2m/4ft), a deciduous, often short-lived perennial, has the clearest aquamarine flowers with yellow stamens. It has a fine structure with rosettes of oblong, bright green leaves. It enjoys damp, shady locations and combines well with *Hosta* 'Blue Moon'.

NEPETA sp. (catmint) These are excellent flowers for growing *en masse* with their lavender to bright blue colours that often last through the summer. Most are attractive to bees, but a disadvantage, as their name suggests, is that they are popular with cats. *N. sibirica* and *N.* 'Six Hills Giant' are tall varieties, to 90cm (3ft) high.

directory

<u>*OPHIOPOGON PLANISCAPUS*</u>
<u>'Nigrescens'</u> (black lilyturf) These ever-green, tufted perennials have all the appearance of grass but produce pinkish-blue flowers on short stems in summer. Grow a block of them for unusual groundcover – they are hardy and in slightly acid, humus-rich soil with sun will spread happily once established; height is around 20cm (8in).

<u>*PHORMIUM TENAX*</u> **Page 176** ◀◀

<u>*TULIPA*</u> 'Queen of Night' With its purple-black colouring this tulip has a special glamour of its own and, though the bulbs are expensive, they look great planted in containers (page 184), grass or *en masse* in a border (bulbs bought from wholesalers are much cheaper). Plant in good, fertile soil and, once the leaves have died down, lift the bulbs to store until it is time to replant.

<u>*VERBENA BONARIENSIS*</u> (syn. *V. patago-nica*) A real wild card in the border with its elegant, structural, almost leafless stems to 2m (6ft) high and panicle-like clusters of small purple flowers all summer; a native of prairies, it looks great *en masse*. A perennial, it is also a good repeat flowerer, but it needs full sun and is not fully hardy.
Page 110 ◀◀

whites and creams

<u>*DELPHINIUM*</u> sp. These architectural plants, ranging in colour from white and pale blue through pinks and purples to deepest blue-black, give height to a planting scheme – the largest are over 2m (6ft) – and look great in block plantings. They need sharp soil in a sheltered site in sun and usually need staking.

<u>*DICENTRA SPECTABILIS*</u> f. *alba* Of great value in that it is both one of the earliest herbaceous plants to flower and that it continues flowering into early summer. Its fine, heart-shaped flowers are borne on arching stems some 60cm (2ft) tall. It has delicate, mid-green leaves and enjoys light shade.

<u>*DIGITALIS PURPUREA*</u> f. *alba* A short-lived biennial (best sown annually) with a wonderful spire 1-2m (3-6ft) high of handsome, tubular flowers. It does best in humus-rich soil in semi-shade, but will grow virtually anywhere.
Page 144 ◀◀

<u>*HELLEBORUS ORIENTALIS* (Lenten rose)</u>, *H. niger* (Christmas rose) Clump-forming perennials, best grown in groups, with white, pale green and pink flowers appearing from mid-winter, to 45cm (18in) in height. Soil requirements vary, but all enjoy dappled shade. *H. foetidus* has dark green leaves with sprays of palest green, cup-like flowers in late winter.

grasses

Flowering ornamental grasses give almost year-round pleasure, both as accent or massed plants that give movement in the slightest breeze and for their winter colouring of brownish and silvery stems. *Clockwise, from top*: *Miscanthus sinensis*; *Elymus hispidis* with *Carex elata;* two kinds of *Cortaderia selloana*, familiarly known *as* pampas grass: 'Pumila' and 'Sunningdale Silver'; and a fountain grass (*Pennisetum*) (see also page 140).

LILIUM REGALE Of the pure white lilies, this and L. 'Casa Blanca' are among the most fragrant and sumptuous, and grow to 1.2m (4ft). L. regale is among the easiest to grow: plant bulbs in sharp sand in well-drained soil; they like full sun but a cool root-run. Lilies can also be container-grown. Page 184 ◀◀

PULMONARIA OFFICINALIS 'Sissinghurst White' An early spring, pure white-flowering plant (the species has pink and blue flowers) with shapely green leaves spotted white or silver. As new foliage is produced following flowering, this is a great plant for edging borders, especially in a shady location. It works well planted with hostas and Solomon's seal (Polygonatum).

ROSA 'Iceberg' In the classic tradition of finely shaped, long-flowering roses, this white rose has lovely olive-green foliage, which, like that of R. glauca (right), makes it a plus even outside the flowering season.

ZANTEDESCHIA AETHIOPICA 'Crowborough' (arum lily) These plants, from lake margins in East Africa, have a stately appearance with huge, white, cup-like flowers (spathes) on long stems to 1m (3ft) high; they are a great addition to a water feature.

hot reds, pinks, yellow & orange

DAHLIA sp. These mid- to late-summer and autumn flowerers are available in a multitude of colours but it is the dark reds and oranges that are the most captivating – especially planted in deep blocks of slightly varying shades for a tapestry effect.

Dahlias range from 60cm (2ft) to 1.2m (4ft) or more; 'bedding' dahlias need no staking and the growing point is pinched out to encourage bushiness. Single and semi-double 'peony' flowers, such as D. 'Bishop of Llandaff', are popular. All require fertile, humus-rich soil in sun.

ESCHSCHOLZIA CALIFORNICA (Californian poppy) Bright or burnt-orange and yellow, fragile-looking flowers and finely divided, fern-like leaves (similar to Artemisia 'Powis Castle') look wonderful planted in drifts and are mat-forming. It is also good for a gravel garden. An annual, it grows 45cm (18in) high and likes poor soil and full sun (the petals close in dull weather).

KNIPHOFIA CAULESCENS (red hot poker, torch lily) This is an ever-green perennial from southern Africa with arching, grass-like leaves. It produces poker-like flowers with a yellow base and orangey tips on thick woody, brown stems, to 1.2m (4ft) high, making an impact in any border.

MACLEAYA CORDATA 'Kelway's Coral Plume' (plume poppy). A stately plant with tall stems of greyish-green leaves to 2.2m (7ft) or more and lovely, feathery coral-pink plumes on slender, branching stems. It spreads by rhizomes and can become invasive.

MONARDA DIDYMA (bee balm, bergamot) Originally from North America, this is an invaluable clump-forming perennial with mid-green pointed leaves, and grows up to 90cm (3ft) high. It has striking, shaggy bright scarlet or pink flowers that appear from midsummer through to autumn. It needs reasonably fertile, well-drained soil and sun or light shade.

NERINE BOWDENII This autumn-flowering bulb from South Africa has attractive bright pink sprays of funnel-shaped flowers. There is a white form (N.b. f. alba), although the flowers are often flushed pale pink. It grows to 45cm (18in) high, and has strap-shaped leaves which need a protective mulch in cold areas.

183

ROSA GLAUCA (syn. R. rubrifolia). A vigorous species rose, reaching to nearly 2m (6ft) in height, and grown mainly for its beautiful, soft bluish-green, burgundy-veined foliage with a plum-like blush; a wonderful addition to a mixed shrub plant-ing. It bears rose-pink flowers in small clusters in summer, followed by lovely round, red hips.

SEDUM SPECTABILE and cultivars (ice plant) These are wonderfully useful plants for long-lasting colour into autumn, as they form solid clumps of pink, ranging from the purest white 'Iceberg' through the pale pink of the species to the glowing dark mauve-pink of 'Brilliant' or 'September Glow'. They have fleshy, grey-green, scalloped leaves and are also attractive to bees.

TAGETES sp. (African marigold, French marigold) These brilliant, profusely flowering plants, often with daisy-like heads ranging from pale yellow through gold to deep red, are great as border or edging plants. Grow in well-drained, fertile soil in full sun. Page 112 ◀◀

suppliers & useful addresses

LONDON DECKING COMPANY
1 Dockhead Wharf
4 Shad Thames
London SE1

M & M TIMBER COMPANY
Hunt House Sawmills
Clows Top
Worcestershire DY14
*decking, trellis, pergolas and
other wooden structures*

MARSTON AND LANGINGER LTD
192 Ebury Street
London SW1
conservatories

PATIO GARDEN CENTRE
100 Tooting Bec Road
London SW17
garden structures and supplies

PORTLAND CONSERVATORIES
Portland House
Ouse Street
Salford, Manchester M5

RAFFLES THATCHED
GARDEN BUILDINGS
Laundry Cottage
Prestwold
Loughborough LE12

REDWOOD DECKING AND
LANDSCAPES LTD
Bridge Inn Nurseries
Moss Side
Formby, Merseyside L37

SANDHILL (BULLION) BAMBOOS
Merchant Trading Department
P O Box 11
Wetherby, West Yorkshire LS22
*bamboo structures and
supplies*

STUART GARDEN
ARCHITECTURE
Burrow Hill Farm
Wiveliscombe
Somerset TA4
structures and advice

Containers, sculpture, specialist products & finishes

AK RUBBER SUPPLIES LTD
6D Parsonage Farm Estate
Stansted, Essex CM24
rubber and industrial matting

BARBARY POTS LTD
45 Fernshaw Road
London SW10

THE BULBECK FOUNDRY
Reach Road
Burwell, Cambridgeshire CB5
metalwork

CHRISTINE-ANN RICHARDS
PLANTERS
Chapel House
The Street, Wanstow
Shepton Mallet
Somerset BA4

CAPITAL GARDEN PRODUCTS
Gibbs Reed Barn
Pashley Road
Ticehurst, East Sussex TN5
fountains, urns and planters

CFS FABRICANT
15 Norwich Road Industrial
Estate
Watton, Norfolk IP25
*powder coating and
steel fabricants*

CONNOISSEUR SUNDIALS LTD
Lane's End
Strefford, Craven Arms
Shropshire SY7

DAVID HARBER SUNDIALS
The Sundial Workshop
Lower Colham Farm
Aston, Oxfordshire RG9

EXTERIOR TIMBER PRODUCTS
48 Faloun Road
London SW2

FAIRWEATHER SCULPTURE
Hillside House
Starston, Norfolk IP20

ANDREW GRACE SCULPTURES
49 Bourne Lane
Much Hadham
Hertfordshire SG10

HANNAH PESCHAR
SCULPTURE GARDEN
Black and White Cottage
Standon Lane
Ockley, West Sussex

LUXCRETE LTD
Premier House
Disraeli Road
London NW10
glass bricks, pavement lights

PILKINGTON PLC
Selwyn House
Cleveland Row
London SW1
*glass manufacturers
and suppliers*

POTS AND PITHOI
The Barns
East Street
Turners Hill
West Sussex RH10

PRESTIGE FINISHERS
19 Wadsworth Road
Perivale, Middlesex
powder coating and enamelling

SANDRIDGE HOUSE
SCULPTURES
Sandridge Hill
Melksham
Wiltshire SN12

SURESET UK LTD
Unit 5
Deverill Road Trading Estate
Sutton Very
Warminster, Wiltshire BA12
*glass chippings and
specialist surfaces*

THE WHICHFORD POTTERY
Whichford
Shipston on Stour
Warwickshire CV36

WOODHAMS LTD
Unit 3, McKay Trading Estate
248-300 Kensal Road
London W10
*galvanized containers, stone
balls, pots and garden
accessories*

Water features & irrigation systems

ANTHONY ARCHER-WILLS
AQUATIC SUPPLIES
Broadford Bridge Road
West Chiltington
West Sussex RH20

BABYLON ARTS
4d Lithos Road
Hampstead, London NW3
water features

CASCADE WATER GARDENS
New Bank Garden Centre
Bury Road
Radcliffe, Manchester M26
all water products

CITY IRRIGATION
Bencewell Granary
Oakley Road
Bromley Common, Kent BR2
all irrigation system supplies

HARTLAND IRRIGATION
Unit 4 Manor Farm Business
Centre
Kingston Lisle
Wantage, Oxfordshire OX12

H2O IRRIGATION
Formula House
West Haddon
Northamptonshire NN6

POROUS PIPE
P O Box 2
Colne, Lancashire BB8
hose and irrigation systems

STAPELEY WATER GARDENS
Stapeley
Natwich, Cheshire CW5
*water feature and irrigation
advice and supplies*

WATER TECHNIQUES
Downside Mill
Cobham, Surrey KT11
irrigation and water systems

Exterior lighting products

JOHN CULLEN LIGHTING
55 King's Road
London SW6

GARDEN AND SECURITY
LIGHTING
23 Jacob Street
London SE16

OUTDOOR LIGHTING
SUPPLIES
3 Kingston Business Centre
Fullers Way South
Chessington, Surrey KT9

LOUIS POULSEN LIGHTING LTD
Surrey Business Park
Weston Road
Epsom, Surrey KT17

TIFFANY LIGHTING LTD
3 Kinnerton Street
London SW1X
neon lighting

Garden furniture, equipment & accessories

APPEAL BLINDS LTD
6 Vale Lane
Bedminster, Bristol BS3

BARNSLEY HOUSE FURNITURE
Barnsley House
Cirencester
Gloucestershire GL7

BROOKGATE DESIGNS
Brookgate Farm Oast
Hurst Green
East Sussex TN1
furniture and equipment design

CONTINENTAL AWNINGS
Unit 14 Torbay Trading Estate
New Road, Brixham
Devon TQ5

PETER DUDGEON FURNITURE
Brompton Place
London SW13

FACTORY FURNITURE
DESIGNS LTD
The Stable Yard
Coles Hill, Swindon SN6

186

GAZE BURVILL BENCHES
Plain Farm Old Dairy
East Tisted
Alton, Hampshire GU34

JUDY GREEN'S GARDEN
STORE
11 Flask Walk
London NW3
*assorted garden accessories
and equipment*

GREENE'S GARDEN
FURNITURE
Lower Farm House
Preston
Wallingford
Oxfordshire OX10

HEVINGHAM COLLECTION
FURNITURE
Weston Down
Weston Colley
Micheldever
Hampshire SO21

IAIN MCGREGOR DESIGNS
Greenbank
West End
Gordon, Berwickshire TD3
furniture and garden supplies

INDIAN OCEAN TRADING
COMPANY
28 Ravenswood Road
London SW12
*garden accessories
and equipment*

INDIAN OCEAN TRADING
COMPANY
155-163 Balham Hill
London SW12
teak supplies and furniture

IRONART OF BATH
61 Walcot Street
Bath BA1
*metal sculpture, furniture and
garden accessories*

INTERDESIGN
Chelsea Harbour Design Centre
Chelsea Harbour
London SW10
furniture and designs

JUNGLE GIANTS
Plough Farm
Wigmore, Herefordshire HR6
*garden accessories, furniture
and supplies*

LLOYD LOOM FURNITURE
Wardentree Lane
Pinchbeck, Spalding
Lincolnshire PE11

THE OAK BARREL COMPANY
Yew Tree House
Nuneaton Road
Over Whiteacre, Coleshill
Warwickshire B46

PEARSON LLOYD FURNITURE
39-41 Folgate Street
London E1
industrial and furniture design

SPENCER FUNG
ARCHITECTURE
3 Pine Mews, London NW3
*garden accessories and
furniture*

SUMMIT FURNITURE
198 Ebury Street
London SW1

Plants, trees and shrubs

APPLE COURT
Hordle Lane
Hordle
Lymington, Hampshire SO41
*grasses, ferns and South
American plants*

ARCHITECTURAL PLANTS
Cooks Farm
Nuthurst
Horsham, West Sussex RH13
*major plants and
specimen plants*

AUSFERN NURSERIES
Tytherleigh House
Hubert Road
Brentwood, Essex CM14
antipodean plants and ferns

DAVID AUSTIN ROSES
Bowling Green Lane
Albrighton
Wolverhampton WV7

PETER BEALES ROSES
London Road
Attleborough, Norfolk NR17

BLOOMS OF BRESSINGHAM
Bressingham
Diss, Norfolk IP22
*alpines, conifers
and perennials*

BRITISH WILD FLOWER
PLANTS LTD
23 Yarmouth Road
Ormesby St Margarets
Great Yarmouth, Norfolk IP22

JOHN CHAMBERS WILD
FLOWER SEEDS
15 Westleigh Road
Barton Seagrave
Kettering
Northamptonshire NN15

THE BETH CHATTO GARDEN
Elmstead Market
Colchester CO7
specialist perennials

THE CITRUS CENTRE
Marehill Nursery
West Mare Lane
Pulborough
West Sussex RH20

CLIFTON NURSERIES
5a Clifton Villas
London W9
wide range of plants and shrubs

DEACON'S NURSERY
Moor View
Godshill, Isle of Wight PO38
fruit bushes and trees

DRYSDALE GARDEN EXOTICS
Bowerwood Road
Fordingbridge
Hampshire SP6
*bamboos and
Mediterranean plants*

EMORSGATE SEEDS LTD
The Pea Mill
Market Lane
Terrington St Clements
King's Lynn PE34
grasses and wildflowers

FIBREX NURSERIES
Honeybourne Road
Pebworth
Stratford on Avon CV37
ferns and ivies

GLOBAL ORANGE GROVES
Edgarton Road
Canford Heath
Poole, Dorset BH17

HARDY'S COTTAGE
GARDEN PLANTS
The Field, Priory Lane
Freefolk Priors
Whitchurch, Hampshire RG28

HOECROFT PLANTS
Severals Grange
Wood Norton
Dereham, Norfolk NR20
grasses and foliage

IDEN CROFT HERBS
Frittenden Road
Staplehurst, Kent TN12

JEKKA'S HERB FARM
Rose Cottage
Shellards Lane
Alveston, Bristol BS12

LANDFORD TREES
Landford Lodge
Salisbury, Wiltshire SP5
specialist trees

LANGLEY BOXWOOD NURSERY
Langley Court
Rake, Liss
Hampshire GU33
topiary and boxwood

MATTOCKS ROSES
The Rose Nurseries
Nuneham Courtenay
Oxford OX44

KEN MUIR
Honeypot Farm
Rectory Road
Weeley Heath
Essex CO16
fruit bushes and trees

THE PALM CENTRE
563 Upper Richmond Road West
London SW14
palms and bamboos

P W PLANTS LTD
Sunnyside
Heath Road
Kenninghall, Norfolk NR16
bamboos and grasses

READS NURSERY
Hales Hall
Loddon, Norfolk NR14
fruit and citrus trees

THE ROMANTIC GARDEN
NURSERY
The Street
Swannington
Norwich NR9
topiary and boxwood

SUFFOLK HERBS
Monks Farm
Cogeshall Road
Kelveden, Essex CO5

TREVOR SCOTT
Thorpe Park Cottage
Thorpe le Soken
Essex CO16
grasses

WYEVALE NURSERIES
Bagshot Road
Chobham, Surrey GU24
bamboos

WOODHAMS WEBSITE:
at http://www.woodhams.co.uk for
further details on what we can achieve
for you, with examples of our work,
effects and displays, many of which
incorporate our merchandise, including
a selection of our tied bunches,
bouquets, plants and floral displays.
Woodhams Landscapes Ltd: survey,
design, build and maintenance of
contemporary gardens from balconies
to large country estates; styles range
from modern, minimal and contemporary to traditional.
Woodhams Ltd Merchandise: for contemporary perspex, glass, metal and
wooden containers as well as classic
creamware, porcelain, metalware and
glass vessels; these and other products can be ordered through our store
or head office.
Woodhams Floral Events: our floral
department create unusual and breath-
taking displays for a range of occa-
sions, from small intimate dinner
parties to weddings, Barmitzvahs,
launches, film premieres.
All enquiries: (+44) 020 8964 9818

Woodhams at One Aldwych: flagship
store in central London offering a
variety of services including floral
orders for companies, stores, restaurants and individuals (Woodhams
flowers and plants, with or without
containers, for delivery across London).
On show are some of our floral
creations and a selected range of our
products.
Enquiries: (+44) 020 7300 0777

Acacia delabata (mimosa) 176
Acanthus spinosus 175
Acer (maple) 52, 94, 176
   griseum 51, 176
   palmatum 55, 92, 93, 176, 178
African marigold (Tagetes) 183
Agapanthus 181
Agave americana (century plant) 175
Akebia quinata (chocolate vine) 186
Alchemilla mollis (ladies' mantle) 81, 180
aluminium 134, 161, 165
Anchusa azurea (syn. A. italica) 181
angel's trumpets (Brugmansia) 113
Anthemis nobile (camomile) 161
aquaria 9, 18, 19
Aralia japonica see Fatsia japonica
arches 26, 29, 33, 163
Artemisia (wormwood) 40, 48, 73, 74, 110, 175, 180
artifical flowers 107
arum lily (Zantedeschia aethiopica) 94, 183
Asplenium scolopendrium (hart's tongue fern) 175
Astelia chathamica 175
Astrantia major 181
awnings 84, 105, 128, 173
azalea 49

Backbone planting 178-9
Baillie, Jonathan 52
balconies 78, 108, 137-8
Ballota 180
balustrades 92, 154
bamboo 34, 39, 101, 103, 105, 133, 142
   (Arundinaria) 118, 180
   (Phyllostachys) 94, 176
   structural 49, 91, 108, 154-5, 157
barbecues 115, 120, 121
bark chippings 161
Barragan, Luis 49
bay (Laurus nobilis) 64, 179
bee balm (Monarda didyma) 183
beech (Fagus sylvatica) 42, 157, 179
benches 87, 92, 101, 131, 148, 149
Berberis thunbergii 40, 52, 178
bergamot (Monarda didyma) 183
bergenia 73, 74
Betula utilis (Himalayan birch) 51, 176

black lilyturf (Ophiopogon planiscapus) 182
blinds 173
blockwork 61, 101, 103, 154
blue fescue (Festuca glauca) 46, 94, 110, 134, 165, 175, 180
Blue-fan palm (Brahea armata) 78, 133, 175
bougainvillea 66
boulders 21, 153
boundaries 63, 66, 82, 152-7
box (Buxus) 30, 48, 101, 128, 130, 157, 178
   clipped 70, 75, 85, 101, 103, 128, 133, 138, 145, 147, 148, 157
   hedging 40, 42, 157
   roof garden 142, 143, 145, 147
Boyd, Arabella Lennox 143
Brachyglottis (syn. Senecio greyi) 44, 73, 110, 138, 180
Bradley-Hole, Christopher 128
Brahea armata (hesper palm) 78, 133, 175
bricks 73, 75, 113, 153
paving 26, 44, 69, 74, 159
bridges 94, 115, 117
bronze fennel (Foeniculum vulgare) 52, 175
Brookes Stacey Randall 18
Brugmansia (angel's trumpets) 113
Bulaitis, Bonita 51
busy lizzies (Impatiens) 103, 104, 131, 149
Buxus (box)
microphylla 178
sempervirens 101, 128, 157, 178
see also box

Cacti 130, 133, 176
Californian poppy (Eschscholzia californica) 181, 183
camomile (Chamaemelum nobile) 161
canals see channels
Canna hybrids 175
canopies 33, 154
   see also awnings
cardoon (Cynara cardunculus) 51, 175
Carex 166, 182
Carpinus betulus (hornbeam) 29, 42, 157, 178
Caryopteris clandonensis 110
catmint (Nepeta) 87, 181
Cedrus
atlantica 46
deodara 92, 176
century plant (Agave americana) 175

Chamaemelum nobile (camomile) 161
channels 33, 63, 107, 115, 166-7
see also rills
cherry, flowering 94, 99, 104
Chinese gardens 9
chocolate vine (Akebia quinata) 186
Choisya ternata 110
Christmas rose (Helleborus niger) 182
Cineraria maritima 133
Cistus 74
Clark, Bob 29
Clematis 81, 157, 186
climbing hydrangea (Hydrangea petiolaris) 186
cobbles 44, 47, 159
   see also pebbles
colour 39, 48–55, 61, 85, 118, 127
   green 81, 110
   purple 73, 81
   silver/grey 31, 73, 81, 85, 108, 110
   white 97, 101, 103, 113, 131
   minimalism 91–3, 97, 103
columns 163
concrete 44, 113, 153, 159-60, 165
Conithus arboreus 176
conservatories 81, 85, 120, 123, 131, 135
containers 93, 103, 105, 110, 131, 133, 145, 165-6, 186
   see also planters; pots
coping 168
copper 52, 91, 155, 165
coral plume (Macleaya cordata) 51
cordyline 127
corrugated sheeting 153
Cortaderia selloana (pampas grass) 182
Corylus (hazel) 117, 176
Cotinus coggyria (smoke bush) 177, 178
cotton lavender (Santolina chamaecyparissus (syn. S. incana) 42, 48, 51, 64, 69, 70, 73, 75, 85, 87, 175, 181
courtyards 77, 84-5, 123
Crambe maritima (sea kale) 74
Cupressus sempervirens (Italian Cypress) 177
curry plant (Helichrysum Italicum) 180
cyclamen 104
Cynara cardunculus (globe artichoke, cardoon) 51, 175
cypress, Italian (Cupressus sempervirens) 39, 177

Dahlia 45, 107, 183
Datura (Brugmansia) 113
decking 93, 104, 113, 118, 160
decorative finishes 168
Delaney, Topher 51
Delphinium 181, 182
Dicentra spectabilis 182

Dicksonia antarctica (tree fern) 177
Digitalis purpurea f. alba (white foxgloves) 48, 145, 182

Echeveria 49
edgings 168
Edmund, Diane 16
Elaeagnus 179
Elymus hispidis 182
Eryngium 110, 175, 181
Eschscholzia californica (Californian poppy) 181, 183
Eucalyptus 138, 177
Euphorbia (spurge) 48, 180
evening primrose (Oenothera biennis) 74
evergreens 91, 92, 101, 105, 118, 141

Fagus sylvatica (beech) 42, 157, 179
Fatsia japonica (Japanese aralia) 118, 142, 175
features 26, 64, 118, 162-8
fencing 47, 49, 155, 156
Feng Shui 94, 108
ferns 48
Festuca glauca (blue fescue) 46, 94, 110, 165, 175, 180
Ficus carica (common fig) 78, 110, 177
fig (Ficus carica) 78, 110, 177
flooring 91, 127, 148, 161
Foeniculum vulgare 'Purpureum' (bronze fennel) 52, 175
Foster, Sir Norman 8
fountains 26, 33, 101, 108, 166, 167
foxgloves (Digitalis purpurea) 48, 145, 182
frames 30, 31, 33
French marigold (Tagetes) 183
furniture 68, 73, 78, 84, 147, 148, 169-73
   see also benches; seating; tables

Galvanized metal 101, 113, 127, 128, 131, 141
   containers 9, 103, 128, 131, 133, 149, 165
   sheeting 134, 153
gazebos 18, 30, 163
geraniums 55
gingko 99, 104
glass 29, 91, 165
aquaria 9, 18, 19
   flooring 104, 131, 134, 159, 161
   screening 31, 52, 133, 141, 154, 155
   walls 46, 125, 127, 128, 131
   water features 103, 104
glass-fibre planters 47, 110
Glechoma hederacea variegata (ground ivy) 32
globe artichoke (Cynara cardunculus) 51, 175

Goldsworthy, Andy 12, 13
granite 29, 34, 44, 152, 159
grass 32, 40, 75, 82, 133, 143
see also lawns
grasses 82, 94, 113, 118, 142,
    182
    colour 64, 73, 74
    sound 34, 37
    texture 51
    *see also Carex; Cortaderia
    selloana; Elymus hispidis;
    Festuca glauca; Miscanthus
    sinensis; Pennisetum*
gravel 43, 49, 127, 133, 143,
    159-60
    minimal gardens 91, 93, 94, 97,
    105
    planted gardens 74, 75, 82
ground cover 63, 94
ground ivy (*Glechoma hederacea
    variegata*) 32
guelder rose (*Viburnum opulus*)
    178
guttering 168

Hamamelis mollis (Chinese witch
    hazel) 52, 177, 178
hammocks 78, 173
hanging pots 137
hart's tongue fern (*Asplenium
    scolopendrium*) 175
hazel (*Corylus*) 176
heathers 104
Hebe vernicosa (hebe) 179
Hedera helix (ivy) 179
hedging 42, 157, 179
Helichrysum 73, 74, 138, 180
Helleborus 48, 180, 182
helxine (*Soleirolia soleirolii*) 77,
    127
herbs 77, 87, 110, 130, 133
Herzog and de Meuron 21
hesper palm (*Brahea armata*) 78,
    133, 175
Heuchera micrantha 181
Himalayan birch, (*Betula utilis*) 51,
    176
Hippophae rhamnoides (sea
    buckthorn) 74, 75
Hobbs, Tom 54
holly (*Ilex*) 157, 179
holm oak (*Quercus ilex*) 74, 75,
    141-2, 148, 178
honeysuckle (*Lonicera japonica*)
    157, 186
hops 52, 157
horizon 61, 64, 66
hornbeam (*Carpinus betulus*) 29,
    42, 157, 178
Hosta 61, 94, 180, 183
hot tubs 108, 166, 167
hyacinths 104, 131, 133
Hydrangea petiolaris (climbing
    hydrangea) 33, 133, 186

Ilex (holly) 157, 179
Impatiens (busy lizzies) 103, 104,
    131, 149
industrial materials 9
iroko 93, 101, 145, 147, 149, 160
irrigation 105

Islamic gardens 33, 107
ivy (*Hedera helix*) 48, 99, 179
    ground cover 94, 101, 103
    screening 145, 148, 157
    walls 63, 81, 85, 87, 104

Japanese gardens 8-9
jasmine 81, 113
Jekyll, Gertrude 8, 52
Juniperus scopulorum 42, 138,
    157, 177

Kitchen gardens 77
Kniphofia caulescens (red hot
    poker, torch lily) 183

Ladies' mantle (*Alchemilla mollis*)
    81, 180
lamb's ears (*Stachys byzantina*)
    51, 181
laurel (*Prunus lusitanica*) 157, 179
laurustinus (*Viburnum tinus*) 179
Laurus nobilis (bay) 64, 179
Lavandula (lavender) 40, 42, 61,
    64, 73, 110, 133, 181
lavatera (*Malva sylvestris*) 74
lavender (*Lavandula*) 40, 42, 61,
    64, 73, 110, 133, 181
lawns 93, 94, 161
Lennox-Boyd, Arabella 42
Lenten rose (*Helleborus orientalis*)
    182
levels 94
lighting 37, 99, 101, 118, 123,
    133-5, 147, 148, 171-2
    fibre optics 17, 171
    uplighters 43, 75, 103, 145,
    147
Ligustrum (privet) 40, 42, 48, 78,
    138, 157, 179
lilies 46, 133, 183, 186
Lilium (lilies) 46, 133, 183, 186
limes, pleached 39, 42, 85, 87,
    96
limestone 9, 78, 91, 92, 154
    features 12, 13, 94, 104, 105
    paving 43, 46, 47, 101, 110,
    160
Liquidambar styraciflua (sweet
    gum) 177, 178
Lloyd, Christopher 52
Lonicera (honeysuckle) 157, 186
Lutsko, Ron 63, 64

Mclarens 8
Macleaya cordata (plume poppy)
    51, 147, 148, 183
Magnolia grandiflora 51, 64, 78,
    179
Mahonia japonica 94
Malva sylvestris (lavatera) 74
maple *see Acer*
marble slabs 161
Meconopsis betonicifolia (blue
    poppy) 181
Mendoza, Jeff 42, 91, 138, 141,
    143
metal 91
    features 37, 94, 133, 143

flooring 9, 127, 130, 131, 134,
    135, 159
    screens, fences, gates 46, 63,
    133, 154, 155, 156
mimosa (*Acacia delabata*) 176
'mind your own business' *see*
    helxine
minimalism 9, 14, 40, 61, 63, 78,
    91–105
mirrors 31-3, 37, 64, 131, 133,
    134, 154, 163
Miscanthus sinensis 94, 175, 182
mock orange 110
Mogul gardens 9
Monarda didyma (bee balm,
    bergamot) 183
Monterey pine (*Pinus radiata*) 177
morning glory 35, 157
moss 158
Mountain flax (*Phormium*) 55, 61,
    118, 176

Nebulgarten 12
Nepeta (catmint) 87, 181
Nerine bowdenii 183
Nerium oleander (rose bay) 177
New Zealand flax (*Phormium*) 55,
    61, 118, 176
Nicotiana sylvestris 181
Nyssa sylvatica 177, 178

Oak (*Quercus ilex*) 74, 75,
    141–2, 148, 178
obelisks 163
objets trouvés 29
Oenothera biennis (evening
    primrose) 74
Olea europaea (olive) 30, 39, 48,
    63, 81, 84, 85, 96, 138, 142,
    147, 177
oleaster (*Elaeagnus angustifolia*)
    179
olive (*Olea europaea*) 30, 39, 48,
    63, 81, 84, 85, 96, 138, 142,
    147, 177
Onopordum acanthium 175
Ophiopogon 165, 176, 182
ornamental cabbages 133, 149
ostrich eggs 131, 134

Pachysandra 94, 101, 180
palms 43, 64, 65, 66, 78, 133,
    177
Parrotia persica 177, 178
parterres 26, 40
Passiflora caerula (passion flower)
    186
passion flower (*Passiflora caerula*)
    186
paths
    design 31, 32, 64, 69, 94, 101,
    103
    materials 44, 45, 69, 92, 113
pavilions 29, 42, 164
paving
    design 26, 32, 39, 40, 101
    materials 92, 101, 110, 159-60
pear (*Pyrus*) 142, 145, 177
pebbles
    decorative finishes 160, 168

features 37, 114, 133, 145
    dry creek 110, 115, 117
    grille floor 130, 134, 135
    paving 45, 47, 78, 161
    and planting 46, 69, 75, 110
    see also cobbles
Pennisetum 143, 182
penstemons 73, 74
pergolas 29, 33, 39, 40, 81, 107,
    163
Perovskia 175, 181
perspective 26, 29, 31, 33, 64,
    105, 123
Perspex 156
Phoenix canariensis (date palm)
    177
Phormium (New Zealand or
    Mountain flax) 55, 61, 118, 176
Photinia 142
Phyllostachys (bamboo) 94, 176
pine (*Pinus*) 64, 68, 69, 74, 142,
    143, 177
Pinus (pine) 64, 68, 69, 74, 142,
    143, 177
pittosporum 110
plans 74, 88, 104, 120, 134, 148
planters 9, 47, 91, 92, 103, 118,
    165-6
    see also containers; pots
planting schemes 26, 29, 31, 40,
    66, 70, 97, 99, 110, 127, 128,
    143
plants 44, 175-86
    architectural 175-6
    aromatic 34, 110, 161
    climbing 94, 142, 186
    drought tolerant 82
    feature 33, 78, 91, 94, 133,
    176-8
    flowers 180-6
    foliage 44, 47, 48, 180-6
    hedging 42, 157
    herbaceous 63, 81
    salt resistant 70, 74
    screening 64, 157
    structural 42, 178-9
    wind resistant 70, 74
plastic 47, 103, 156, 165
    furniture 103, 104, 105
    pipes 32, 153-4
    see also Perspex;
    polycarbonate
Pleioblastus variegatus (bamboo)
    180
plume poppy (*Macleaya cordata*)
    51, 147, 148, 183
polycarbonate 141, 156
Polygonatum (Solomon's seal)
    183
pools 64, 93, 94, 96, 166
pots 93, 103, 125, 130
    stone 46, 92
    terracotta 30, 39, 49, 52, 70,
    84, 93, 110, 128, 166
    see also containers; planters
powder-coating 155
Privalite glass 134, 155
privet (*Ligustrum*) 40, 42, 48, 78,
    138, 157, 179
Prunus
    lusitanica (laurel) 157, 179
    serrula (ornamental cherry) 51
    subhirtella autumnalis (winter-

flowering cherry) 94
Pulmonaria officinalis 183
pumice 69, 70
Pyrus salicifolia (pear) 177

Quercus ilex (Holm oak) 74, 75, 141–2, 148, 178

Raised beds 48, 87, 93, 113, 165
red hot poker (*Kniphofia caulescens*) 183
rills 26, 29, 33, 64, 94, 101, 104, 107, 127, 141, 164, 166–7
  see also channels
rocks 13, 16, 77, 91, 97, 114
roof coverings 168
roof gardens 47, 91, 137–8, 141, 142, 145
roof terraces 40, 81, 108
Rosa (rose) 183
rose bay (*Nerium oleander*) 177
rosemary (*Rosmarinus officinalis*) 42, 110, 133, 180
roses 46, 183
Rosmarinus officinalis (rosemary) 42, 110, 133, 180
rubber matting 161
rudbeckia 30
Ruta graveolens 181

Sage (*Salvia officinalis*) 40, 42, 52, 73, 181
Salix (willow) 32, 108, 178
salvage items 163
Salvia officinalis (sage) 40, 42, 52, 73, 181
Santolina 42, 48, 51, 64, 69, 70, 73, 75, 85, 87, 110, 175, 181
scent 34, 46, 113
Schwarz, Martha 14, 15, 47
screens 44, 52, 63, 66, 68, 69, 141, 154–7
  fabric 31, 35, 108, 155, 173
  plant 40, 64, 145
sculpture 26, 70, 91, 114, 164
sea buckthorn (*Hippophae rhamnoides*) 74, 75
sea kale (*Crambe maritima*) 74
seating
  built-in 78, 93, 165, 170
  free-standing 69, 131, 165, 170
Sedum 73, 81, 141, 183
Senecio
  cineraria (cineraria) 148, 175, 181
  greyi (*Brachyglottis*) 44, 73, 110, 138, 180
sheds 164
shells 37, 75, 145
showers 108, 167
shrubs 63, 81, 82, 176–8
Silene alba (white campion) 74
silver birch 108
Silvestrin, Claudio 21, 39
slate 9, 91, 125, 158, 159–60
smoke bush (*Cotinus coggyria*) 177, 178
soft furnishings 173
soil retainers 168

Soleirolia soleirolii (helxine) 77, 127
Solomon's seal (*Polygonatum*) 183
Sorbus aria (whitebeam) 178
sound 34, 37, 108, 162
spas 166
spouts 167
spurge (*Euphorbia*) 48, 180
Stachys byzantina (lamb's ears) 51, 181
star jasmine (*Trachelospermum jasminoides*) 81, 113, 127, 148, 186
statice 37
steam 12, 162
steps 94, 101, 103, 104, 108, 164
stone 31, 69, 70, 87, 91, 154
  benches 39, 120
  containers 165-6
  features 14, 24, 31, 69–70, 94, 96, 120, 141, 162
  paving 48, 81, 121, 125, 160
  walls 87, 97, 154
  reconstituted 87, 159
storage 101, 117, 141, 170
succulents 74, 176
summer houses 164
sundials 81, 164
surface materials 94, 158-61
sweet gum (*Liquidambar styraciflua*) 177, 178
swimming pools 61, 94, 108, 110, 167

Tables 26, 147, 170
Tagetes (African/French marigold) 183
Taxus baccata (yew) 157, 179
terraces 69, 99, 101, 105, 120, 145
terracotta 30, 39, 49, 52, 70, 84, 93, 110, 114, 128, 166
thyme (*Thymus*) 110, 161
tiles 125, 153, 158, 161
timber 93, 115, 118, 120, 154, 160, 166
  flooring 118, 125, 147, 149
  see also named species
Tingiringi Gum (*Eucalyptus glaucescens*) 177
topiary 26, 29, 40, 42, 81, 94, 103, 133, 157, 179
torch lily (*Kniphofia caulescens*) 183
Trachelospermum jasminoides (star jasmine) 81, 113, 127, 148, 186
tree ferns (*Dicksonia antarctica*) 177
tree peonies 118
trees 29, 63, 103, 107, 138, 142
  espaliered 81, 142, 145, 157
  exotic 82
  feature 47, 107, 176–8
  pleached 39, 42, 81, 85, 87, 157
trellis 31, 78, 82, 145, 147, 154, 156, 157
Trillium grandiflorum 48
trompe l'oeil 123
troughs 34, 103, 141

tulips 182, 186

Umbrellas 173
urns 33, 70, 74, 93

Valode and Pistre 51
vegetables 77
verbascum 51
Verbena bonariensis (syn. *V. patagonica*) 51, 182
Versailles box 166
Viburnum 74, 75, 157, 178, 179
vine 61, 186
vistas 20, 26, 29, 64, 69
Vitis coignetiae (vine) 61, 186
Voysey, Charles 47

Walkways 128
walled gardens 77
walls 26, 64, 78, 81, 82, 101
  colour 39, 49, 51–2, 91, 97, 127, 154
  curved 44, 46–7
water 2, 10, 114, 115, 165, 166–7
  features 42, 81, 90–7, 99–105, 108, 118–21, 134, 166–7
    as containers 165
    see also channels; rills
  Mogul gardens 107
  mood 34, 37
  perspective 26, 29, 33
  sanctuary 78, 82, 134
  sound 107–8
  texture 51
  vista 29, 64, 65
watering systems 142–3
white campion (*Silene alba*) 74
whitebeam (*Sorbus aria*) 178
wicker baskets 96
willow (*Salix*) 32, 108, 178
  plaited, screens 44, 45
  trellis 30, 157
  woven
    containers 166
    fences 55, 82, 92
    hurdles 66, 69, 155
    panels 70, 74, 153, 154, 156
wind chimes 108, 118
windbreaks 69, 70, 75
wire mesh 141
Wisteria 147, 148, 163, 186
witch hazel (*Hamamelis mollis*) 52, 177, 178
wood *see* timber
wormwood (*Artemisia*) 180

Yew (*Taxus baccata*) 42, 96, 103, 104, 157, 179
York stone 48, 91, 120, 121, 154, 160
Yucca filamentosa 176

Zantedeschia aethiopica (arum lily) 183
Zen gardens 8, 14, 15, 94
zinc 101

ACKNOWLEDGEMENTS

PHOTOGRAPHIC ACKNOWLEDGEMENTS

1 Andrew Wood;

2 1st row far left Andrew Wood; left landscape artist Dale Joseph Rowe; right Andrew Wood; far right Axiom / Jim Holmes; 2nd row far left The Interior Archive / Herbert Ypma / Architect Manolo Mestre; left, right & far right Andrew Wood; 3rd row Andrew Wood; 4th row far left Clive Nichols; left, right & far right Andrew Wood;

4–7 Andrew Wood;

10 Tony Stone Images / Rene Sheret;

11–12 Andrew Wood;

12–13 Photograph by Andy Goldsworthy / © Andy Goldsworthy / Balanced Rocks – Morecambe Bay, May 1978 from 'Hands to Earth';

14 Earth from Above / Yann Arthus-Bertrand;

15 Martha Schwartz Inc.;

16 Arcaid / John Edward Linden;

16–17 Dyson / sculpture by Diana Edmunds;

18–19 Andrew Wood;

19 Brookes Stacey Randall / Arcblue / Peter Durant;

20 Margherita Spiluttini / architects Herzog & de Meuron;

20–21 Christian Sarramon / Architect Claudio Silvestrin;

22 above Brookes, Stacey, Randall / Arcblue / Peter Durant;

22–23 View / Chris Gascoigne;

25 Andrew Wood;

25 Clive Nichols;

26–28 Andrew Wood;

29 left Clive Nichols / Gordon White, Texas;

29 centre Andrew Wood; right Jerry Harpur / designer Bob Clark, California;

30 Andrew Wood;

31 Jerry Harpur / Dan White & Rule, Sangha & Associates, Vancouver, BC;

32 Andrew Wood;

33 left Dyson / sculpture by Diana Edmunds; right Andrew Wood;

34–37 right Andrew Wood;

38–39 Christian Sarramon / Architect Claudio Silvestrin;

39 Andrew Wood;

40 above Earth From Above / Yann Arthus-Bertrand; below Clive Nichols / Ton Ter Linden, Holland;

41 above Jerry Harpur / designer Berry Garden Company, London; below Agence Top / Robert Tixador / gardens at d'Eyrignac Castle, 24590 Salignac open all year between 1000 and 1900 hours;

42 above Clive Nichols / designer Arabella Lennox-Boyd, Chelsea 1998; below Jerry Harpur / designer Jeff Mendoza, NYC, USA;

42–43 Michael Freeman / Ricardo Legorreta House;

44 above Andrew Wood; below Beatrice Pichon Clarisse / CREDIT?;

44–45 Andrew Wood;

46–47 Martha Schwartz Inc.;

47 above Richard Davies; below Photograph by Andy Goldsworthy / © Andy Goldsworthy 'The Wall went for a Walk' Grizedale, Cumbria;

48 left Axiom / Jim Holmes; right Clive Nichols / Blakedown Landscapes, Chelsea 1998;

49 Tim Street-Porter / Barragan;

50 Gary Rogers;

51 above Clive Nichols / Bonita Bulaitis, Hampton Court; below Archipress / Luc Boegly / landscape architect Kathryn Gustafson;

52 left Clive Nichols / designer Jonathan Baillie; centre Andrew Wood; right Axiom / Jim Holmes;

53 Andrew Lawson / RHS Chelsea 1996, Sally Clarke's Kitchen Garden;

54 Jerry Harpur / designer Tom Hobbs, Vancouver, BC;

55 Andrew Wood;

56 above Jerry Harpur;

56–59 Andrew Wood;

60 Undine Prπhl/Morton / Cordell Architects;

61 Arcaid / John Edward Linden / Architect Richard Meier;

62 Christian Sarramon / architect Claudio Silvestrin;

63 left Andrew Wood; right designer Ron Lutsko;

64 left Andrew Wood; right designer Ron Lutsko;

65 Jerry Harpur / Mr and Mrs Lerner, Rancho Mirage, California, USA;

66 left Arcaid / John Edward Linden; right Andrew Wood;

67 Arcaid / John Edward Linden;

68–73 Andrew Wood;

75 below Andrew Wood;

76–77 Andrew Wood;

78 left Richard Glover / architect John Pawson; right Andrew Wood;

79 The Interior Archive / Herbert Ypma / Architect Manolo Mestre;

80–81 Andrew Wood;

82 above Gross & Daley; below left Andrew Wood; below right Jerome Darblay;

83–89 Andrew Wood;

90 Richard Davies / Hauer-King House, Future Systems;

91 Jerry Harpur / designer Jeff Mendoza, NYC, USA;

92–93 Andrew Wood;

94 left Tim Street-Porter / Architect Richard Neutra; right Tim Street-Porter;

95 Gary Rogers;

96 Andrew Wood;

97 left The Interior Archive / Herbert Ypma/architect Manolo Mestre; right Andrew Wood;

98–100 Andrew Wood;

101 Clive Nichols / Charles Worthington;

102–103 Andrew Wood;

105 below centre Clive Nichols / Charles Worthington; below Clive Nichols / Charles Worthington;

106–111 Andrew Wood;

112–113 Garden Picture Library / Ron Sutherland / Chelsea Flower Show 1996 / You Magazine / Yardley Exhibition;

113–123 Andrew Wood;

123 Elizabeth Whiting & Associates / Rodney Hyett;

124 Studio Verne / Architect Jo Crepain;

125 above sculpture by Diana Edmunds; below Tim Street-Porter / Mondrian Hotel;

126–127 Elizabeth Whiting & Associates / Neil Lorimer;

127 above Vogue Living / John Hay; below Tim Street-Porter;

128 above Clive Nichols / designer Christopher Bradley-Hole, Chelsea 1998; centre Ray Main / Mainstream / Architect Mark Guard; below Arcaid/John Edward Linden / Architect Mark Guard;

128–129 Arcaid/John Edward Linden / Architect Mark Guard;

130–135 Andrew Wood;

136–137 Clive Nichols;

137 Andrew Wood;

138 above Andrew Wood; below Jerry Harpur / designer Jeff Mendoza, NYC, USA;

139 Andrew Wood;

140 Jerry Harpur / designer Jeff Mendoza, NYC, USA;

141 left Jerry Harpur / designer Jeff Mendoza, NYC, USA; right Beatrice Pichon-Clarisse;

142 Tim Street-Porter;

143 above Deidi von Schaewen / Françoise Dorget / architect Charles Chauliagout; below Richard Glover / garden designer Arabella Lennox-Boyd / Le Coq d'Argent, No. 1 Poultry / architect Stirling Wilford;

144–149 Andrew Wood;

152 Axiom / Jim Holmes;

153 top Narratives / Jan Baldwin; centre left Andrew Wood; centre right View / Peter Cook; below Andrew Wood;

154 top & centre Andrew Wood; below left Dominique Vorillon; below centre & right Andrew Wood;

156 above left & centre Andrew Wood; above right Martha Schwartz Inc.; below left & centre Andrew Wood; below right Paul Rocheleau / Architects Arquintectonica;

157 Andrew Wood;

158 The World of Interiors / Bill Batten;

159 above Clive Nichols / designer David Stevens, Chelsea 1998; below far left Andrew Wood; below left Paul White Photography; below right The Interior Archive / Helen Fickling; below far right Paul White Photography;

160 1st row Andrew Wood; 2nd row left Andrew Wood; right Clive Nichols; 3rd row 1st picture Paul Ryan / International Interiors / Paula Pryke & Peter Romanuik; 2nd picture Andrew Wood; 3rd picture Clive Nichols / designer Mark Walker, Chelsea 1998 4th, 5th & 6th pictures Andrew Wood;

161 above left Andrew Wood; above right landscape artist Dale Joseph Rowe; centre & below Andrew Wood;

162 Andrew Wood;

163 above Tim Street-Porter; centre left Andrew Lawson/ RHS Chelsea 1996, Sally Clarke's Kitchen Garden; centre right Jerry Harpur / Arthur Ericksson; below Andrew Wood;

164 above left Marianne Majerus; above centre Clive Nichols / Pat Volk, Hannah Pescher Gallery, Surrey; above right Clive Nichols / David Harber; centre left Andrew Wood; centre left Andrew Wood; below far left Andrew Wood;

acknowledgements

below left Deidi von Schaewen/architect Gilles Bouchez; below right designer Ron Lutsko; below far right Clive Nichols / Gordon White, Austin, Texas;

165 above Andrew Wood; 165 below far left Andrew Wood; 165 below left The Interior Archive / Helen Fickling; below right & far right Andrew Wood;

166 above Clive Nichols / Evening Standard, Chelsea 98; below left Andrew Wood; below centre Jerry Harpur / Chanticleer Garden, Wayne, Pennsylvania; below right Clive Nichols;

167 above left Andrew Wood; above right Clive Nichols / designer Madison Cox, Yves St. Laurent Garden, Chelsea 1997; centre left Andrew Wood; centre right Clive Nichols; below Andrew Wood;

168 above Andrew Wood; centre left & centre Andrew Wood; centre right Jerry Harpur/designer Jeff Mendoza; 168 below Andrew Wood;

169 Andrew Wood;

170 above Andrew Wood; below far left, left & below right Andrew Wood; below far right Clive Nichols;

171 above Andrew Wood; below far left, left & centre Andrew Wood; below right Clive Nichols; below far right Andrew Wood;

172 above far left & left Clive Nichols; above right & far right Andrew Wood; below far left Clive Nichols; below left & right Andrew Wood; below far right Dyson / sculpture by Diana Edmunds;

173 above Andrew Wood; centre right Tim Street-Porter; below left Andrew Wood; bottom left Andrew Lawson/ RHS Chelsea 1996, Sally Clarke's Kitchen Garden; below right Paul Rocheleau / Architects Arquintectonica;

174 Andrew Wood;

175 above left & right Andrew Wood; centre left Clive Nichols; centre right Clive Nichols / Green Farm Plants / Piet Oudolf; below left Clive Nichols; below right Anne Hyde;

176 top Garden Picture Library / Jerry Pavia; above left Clive Nichols; above right Jerry Harpur; centre Anne Hyde; below left David Rosen; below right Clive Nichols / Strybing Arboretum, California;

177 above left Andrew Lawson;

above right Anne Hyde; centre left Anne Hyde; centre right John Glover; below left Clive Nichols; below right Andrew Wood;

178 top left Andrew Wood; top right Anne Hyde; above left Clive Nichols; above right Andrew Wood; centre Anne Hyde; below right Andrew Lawson; below left John Glover;

179 above Clive Nichols; centre Clive Nichols / designers Piet & Anja Oudolf; below & bottom Andrew Wood;

180 top Andrew Wood; above left Marcus Harpur; above right & centre left Andrew Wood; centre right Marcus Harpur; below Andrew Lawson; bottom Andrew Wood;

181 top left Andrew Wood; top right Jerry Harpur; centre Anne Hyde; below left Clive Nichols; below right Clive Nichols; bottom Jerry Harpur; 182 top left Andrew Wood; top right John Glover; above left Clive Nichols / Little Court, Crawley, Hants; 182 centre left Andrew Wood; centre right John Glover; below left Andrew Wood; below centre Clive Nichols / designer Geoff Whitten; below right Andrew Wood; bottom right Andrew Wood;

183 above left Marcus Harpur; above right Clive Nichols; centre Clive Nichols; below left Andrew Wood; below right John Glover; bottom left Andrew Lawson; bottom right Andrew Wood;

184 top left Andrew Wood; top right Andrew Lawson; above left Anne Hyde; centre left John Glover; centre right Clive Nichols; below left Andrew Wood; below centre Clive Nichols; below right Andrew Lawson.

AUTHOR'S ACKNOWLEDGEMENTS

First I would like to thank the team at Quadrille, especially Jane O'Shea, who had the most difficult job of keeping all the balls in the air. Thanks also to Françoise Dietrich, who has once again shown her creativity both on photographic shoots and by her outstanding page designs, which have helped build my signature. Thanks to Alison Freegard, who kept the words flowing; to Stephanie Amor who – along with Judy Dobias and her team at Camron PR – told all the world about this new cutting-edge book; and to Alison Cathie for believing in my philosophy and passion.

Thanks, also, to Andrew Wood for his amazing photography; to Nadine Bazar for her painstaking and inspired picture research; and to Michael Codron for appearing in the book without his equity card.

I would also like to thank my very valued team at work including: Terry Nightingill; my three designers, Kate, Annabel and Isobel; Robin, Heather, Titch, Mark and all the other people who make it possible for me to put a time-consuming project such as this together.

Thanks are also due to David Davies, Anouska Hempel, Carol and Michael Storey, Lawrence Issacson, Mark Watty, Charles Worthington, Alan Peters, Mr and Mrs Woolf, Mr and Mrs Greer, Lady Bonfield, James and Deirdre Dyson, Dee Nolan, Neville Abraham and Ron Lutsko. I would also like to thank all my friends and family for their much-valued support.

PUBLISHER'S ACKNOWLEDGEMENTS

The publishers would like to thank the following: Alison Freegard for her overall editorial guidance and contribution to the text; Helena Attlee, Stephanie Donaldson and Carole McGlynn for additional text and editorial work; Sarah Widdicombe for proofreading; Elizabeth Wiggans for indexing; Caroline Perkins for editorial assistance; Bridget Bodoano and Sarah Jane O'Callaghan for design support and Ken Wilson for his work on the typography and design.